God's Law of ATTRACTION

Revealing the mystery and benefits
of your soul's prosperity.

P A T R I C I A   K I N G

GOD'S LAW OF ATTRACTION
© 2015 Patricia King

Unless otherwise identified, Scripture quotations are taken from the NEW AMERICAN STANDARD BIBLE®, Copyright ©1960, 1962, 1963, 1968, 1971, 1972, 1973, 1975, 1977, 1995 by The Lockman Foundation. Used by permission.

Scripture quotations marked (NKJV) taken from the New King James Version®. Copyright © 1982 by Thomas Nelson. Used by permission. All rights reserved.

Scripture quotations marked (NIV) taken from the Holy Bible, New International Version®, NIV® Copyright ©1973, 1978, 1984, 2011 by Biblica, Inc.® Used by permission. All rights reserved worldwide.

Scripture quotations marked (NLT) taken from Holy Bible. New Living Translation copyright© 1996, 2004, 2007, 2013 by Tyndale House Foundation. Used by permission of Tyndale House Publishers Inc., Carol Stream, Illinois 60188. All rights reserved.

Scripture quotations marked AMP taken from Amplified Bible (AMP) Copyright© 1954, 1958, 1962, 1964, 1965, 1987 by The Lockman Foundation.

Scripture quotations marked (KJV) taken from King James Version. Public Domain

Distributed by:
Patricia King Ministries
PO Box 1017
Maricopa, AZ 85139
PatriciaKing.com

For worldwide distribution.
ISBN: 978-1-621661-69-6

God's Law

of Attraction

Revealing the mystery and benefits
of your soul's prosperity

Endorsements

"What comprises the soul of a person? Is your soul prospering? Does your emotional state draw or repel people, favor and provision? Learn from spiritual pioneer, entrepreneur and stateswoman, Patricia King, about this and much more. This book is highly recommended if you wish to succeed in any area of life and ministry!"

Dr. James W. Goll
Founder of Encounters Network, Prayer Storm
GET eSchool and International Best-Selling Author

"Our world today is hungry for truth. Many people are looking for a way to experience a life of blessings and well-being. While there are multitudes of authors who will promise you success, very few of them hold the keys to a prosperous soul. My dear friend, Patricia King, exemplifies how to live well in her newest book, *God's Law of Attraction*. She paints a Spirit-inspired picture of a healthy soul as she explains how to maintain a vibrant lifestyle grounded in God's purposes and blessings. Patricia unpacks powerful truths of God's Word that will radically change the way you live. This book will take you into the overflow of God's goodness, as His kingdom realities are revealed in your life!"

Dr. Che Ahn
Founding Apostle of H.I.M. Apostolic Network

"Something attracted you to this book. Patricia King walks in an atmosphere that attracts the activity of heaven and that activity attracts people who are hungry for God. You are now part of that experience. Read this book and learn for yourself how to catalyze the power that both attracts and generates divine appointments. As Patricia says in this book, "like attracts like," so it's highly likely that you are called to walk in the same divine law she is experiencing. The New Age movement was excited years ago over a book called *The Secret*, but *God's Law Of Attraction* is the book that should have been read. It's significantly deeper and more practical."

Dr. Lance Wallnau
Lance Learning Group

"In order to attract the life of God, you have to be willing to see it first. It is all a matter of focus. Patricia King invites you to change the way you see in life, so that you can change the outcomes you obtain by faith. *God's Law Of Attraction* is filled with practical nuggets that will ground you in the Scriptures and offer you a pathway to well-being and wholeness in Christ."

Dr. Mark J. Chironna, MA, PhD
Founder of Mark Chironna Ministries

"As you read this book ... stop! Be sure to meditate on the quotes, summaries and activation plan at the end of each chapter. This is a powerful learning technique that will serve to inform and transform your mind. Learn how to activate the power that is available as you master the principles of *God's Law of Attraction*."

Dr. Clarice Fluitt
Author, Motivation Speaker, Transformational Life Coach

"In her new book, *God's Law of Attraction*, Patricia King provides many simple but powerful guidelines for drawing unto yourself the life, relationships, finances and future you so earnestly desire. Follow these guidelines and the activations at the end of each chapter and you too will experience how *God's Law of Attraction* puts every good thing He made within your grasp!"

Dr. Joan Hunter
Author/Evangelist

"Patricia brings a unique and powerful insight to my favorite subject – soul prosperity. By resisting "stinking thinking" and keeping our mind focused on God's goodness and His promises, we become a magnet for blessings to be attracted to our lives. As I have put these powerful precepts to work, I have experienced demonic assignments immediately breaking off, as well as a flow of the presence and provision of God. Let this wonderful book guide you into a life of peace, promises and prosperity of soul."

Katie Souza
Founder of Katie Souza Ministries

"Patricia King does it again by practically and scripturally unpacking a spiritual principle that will revolutionize your entire life! *God's Law of Attraction* is a book that you'll want to share with others around you as you begin to discover the power that's contained within its pages. I believe that you'll begin to experience new favor, blessing and extraordinary miracles as you receive life-changing insight from this wonder-filled book. I know you'll enjoy it as much as I did!"

Joshua Mills
Best-Selling Author, *31 Days to a Miracle Mindset*

"Patricia King's new book, *God's Law of Attraction*, unlocks Bible truths that will help you succeed, flourish and thrive in every area of your life – body, soul and spirit. But don't think of it as simply a "key" – it is much more than that. This book is a divine secret revealed, a spiritual accelerator that will zoom you past life-long blockages and hindrances and quicken you into increased manifestations of faith, favor, provision, joy, peace, power and every good thing you have been given in Christ. When you grab hold of the scriptural revelations, kingdom principles, powerful prayers and activations that Patricia shares, get ready! You won't just be going to a new level, you'll be opening a new realm of divine abundance and dominion authority that you can walk in all the days of your life!"

Robert Hotchkin
XP Ministries

Table of Contents

Dedication

"I dedicate this book to all who are hungry to live in the fullness of God's truth and blessing in their lives."

—Patricia King

CHAPTER ONE

The Secret

"The secret things belong to the Lord our God, but the things revealed belong to us and to our children forever."

—Deuteronomy 29:29 (NIV)

The Secret

In 2006, a book entitled *The Secret* became very popular around the world, following the production of a film by the same name. It was during a difficult time in author Rhonda Byrne's life that she became aware of "The Secret" and discovered, through her research, that many world-renowned figures such as Plato, Shakespeare, Newton, Hugo, Beethoven, Lincoln, Emerson, Edison, and Einstein, as well as many modern-day scientists, philosophers, entrepreneurs and successful leaders had also discovered "The Secret." The more she studied, the more she realized that "The Secret" had been around for a long time and that many people had not only discovered it but, by intentionally applying it to their lives, had experienced great success as a result.

As the book gained world-wide popularity, many famous and everyday people affirmed the power of "The Secret." They testified of healings from physical ailments, diseases and emotional pressures such as depression, tension, stress and anxiety. Some testified of recovering from accidents, calamities and even death-bed illnesses by applying "The Secret." Thousands have credited

"The Secret" for increased wealth and accelerated favor among their peers, bosses, clients and investors.

Others have shared how applying "The Secret" brought them their desired homes, cars, jobs, careers and promotions. Troubled and strained relationships have been restored, lifemates have been found, and businesses have been graced with much needed turnarounds within days of applying "The Secret." Even children have reported attracting the desires of their hearts, such as higher grades and popularity, by using "The Secret." Many doctors, university professors and business owners have shared "The Secret" with their patients, students, employees and clients, observing notable results.

During the height of the book's popularity, however, much of the Christian world was in a bit of upheaval over *The Secret*. Great warnings were sounded concerning the book and the film. I became curious as to what was fueling the opposition. Whenever I asked about people's concerns with "The Secret," all I received back were vague comments like: "It's New Age," or "It's witchcraft," or "It's the doctrine of demons." When pressed for why, no answer was given.

After a while, I decided to buy the book and find out for myself what all the fuss was about. I read the book with care to try and understand why this apparent "secret" for life was attracting so much opposition in the Christian world.

As I read *The Secret*, I could see where the concerns of those who had heralded the warnings were coming from. The book is, after all, a compilation of insights and quotes from motivational speakers, life coaches, New Age teachers and practitioners, secular philosophers, metaphysicians and leaders of various world religions. But, what exactly is "The Secret" they have all discovered?

As I continued to read, I realized that these seekers have simply stumbled upon a God-created law, while the true Author of "The Secret" remains unknown to most of them. They have discovered what science has termed The Law of Affinity or The Law of Attraction. The most simple definition of these is that "like attracts like." However, we will use a more expanded and recognized definition for the purpose of this book:

I attract into my life whatever I give my thoughts, feelings, attention, energy, focus and belief to – whether positive or negative.

The author and contributors of *The Secret* claim that if you align your thoughts and attention to the things you desire, they will be attracted to you. This has been scientifically proven, but is it a "secret" that Christians should embrace and practice?

God Creates Natural Laws, Man Only Discovers Them

"It is the glory of God to conceal a matter, but the glory of kings is to search out a matter."   —Proverbs 25:2

Throughout history, scientists, philosophers, mathematicians, inventors and others have discovered thousands of natural laws. These laws were there all the time. God created them. Humans have only discovered them, named them and learned to use them. For example, The Law of Gravity is a law that God created. What goes up, comes down. The Law of Gravity works for all people all the time, whether they are aware of it or not and whether they are Christians or not. If you are blindfolded, you might not be conscious that a cliff is just steps away, but when you take a step off the edge you will surely discover the effects of the The Law of Gravity – like it or not.

You will not find the term "law of gravity" in the Bible, or even a clear definition of it within its pages, but we know that God created it. And as we observe nature and study the cause and effect of this law, we can confirm that it exists.

The same goes for The Law of Aerodynamic Lift discovered by Sir Isaac Newton. It is an outstanding discovery that we are all grateful for. It is what keeps an airplane in the sky. The law was there all the time. God created it and man discovered it. You will not find the name of this law in the Bible either, but it is still a God-created law for all people to utilize, whether Christian or not.

Likewise, The Law of Attraction is also a God-created law. New-Agers did not create it, God did – and those who were searching, found it. Again, you will not find the term in the Bible, but we can certainly discover truths about The Law of Attraction and its operation within the pages of Scripture and also as we observe the effects of it in our lives.

God's Spirit Is Poured Out Upon All Flesh

Acts 2:17 states that, "'In the last days,' God says, 'I will pour out my Spirit on all people.'" It doesn't say, on all Christians. All mankind has access to the revelation God releases to a generation, but if they do not know the Author they might not apply it for His holy purposes. We can help the world come to know the Author.

Too often, we throw out the baby with the bath water. We need to learn to extract the precious from the worthless and hold fast to that which is good. Let's discover the truth behind "The Secret" that has captured the attention of so many in the world. Let's look for "The Secret" as found in the Scriptures, so that we can understand and apply this Law of Attraction according to God's design and purposes.

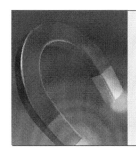

"Sometimes we critically judge what we do not understand and therefore miss the blessing of discovering truth, wisdom and discernment as we search the matter out to see if these things be so."   —Patricia King

Summary

1. God alone is the Creator of laws that govern nature and the universe.

2. Man discovers these laws.

3. God's laws work for all people all the time, whether you are a Christian or not.

4. When we apply God's laws, we will be affected by their results (i.e. The Law of Gravity).

5. The names of many God-created laws are not found or specifically defined in the Scriptures (i.e. The Law of Aerodynamic Lift), but their existence is confirmed.

6. The simple definition of The Law of Attraction is "like attracts like."

7. The more expanded definition we are using for this book is: "I attract into my life whatever I give my thoughts,

feelings, attention, energy, focus and belief to – whether positive or negative."

8. We are to be seekers of truth, extracting the precious from the worthless, looking for "The Secret" as confirmed in the Scriptures according to the Spirit of Truth.

Activation

If you desire to discover God's Law of Attraction and have the blessing of it manifest in your life, pray the following:

Dear Heavenly Father,

I am open to all You desire to reveal to me. I am hungry for You and all that You have for my life. Therefore, I will seek You with all my heart. Please grant me wisdom, revelation and understanding in Your ways as I read this book. Open my heart and mind to The Law of Attraction that You created for my benefit. Reveal to me things I have never understood before and establish these revelations in my life that I might flourish in You and give You glory.

In Jesus' name I pray. Amen.

CHAPTER TWO

Understanding God's Law of Attraction

"Whatever you vividly imagine, ardently desire and enthusiastically act upon will inevitably come to pass."

—Paul J. Meyer, Motivational Speaker

Understanding
God's Law of Attraction

Have you ever noticed that sometimes what you desire or need seems to materialize out of nowhere? Or, perhaps you have been thinking about someone and they suddenly call you, or you see them as you are out and about. Do you know people who live in continual favor? And they appear to have a steady flow of opportunities, blessings, promotion and open doors that others do not?

On the other hand, you are probably aware of people who seem to have one bad break after another. Some are accident prone. Others continue to attract unhealthy relationships. Still others struggle financially – no matter how hard they try.

For the most part, both types of people have attracted those manifestations to themselves – positive or negative – through their thoughts, beliefs, choices, responses and the words they speak. This is The Law of Attraction.

God's laws work for all people, all the time – whether they are conscious of them or not. When you understand this God-created law, you can intentionally create realms of fulfilled desire, blessing and increase in your life, while avoiding realms of adversity and curse. As you partner with the Holy Spirit, you can purposely create your world according to God's blueprint.

The Soul Connection

There is a key verse in Scripture that demonstrates the principle of The Law of Attraction:

> "Beloved, I pray that in all respects you may prosper and be in good health, just as your soul prospers."   —3 John 1:2

Here, John reveals that our health, well-being and prosperity are connected to the prosperity of our soul. This is a huge key for us that should not be passed over quickly. When your thoughts, focus and beliefs are in alignment with God's truth, promises and blessings, your soul prospers. When your soul prospers, you potentially prosper and experience vibrant health in every other area of your life. Why? Because you attract to yourself what your soul thinks on with focus and belief.

To prosper means to grant success; to flourish and thrive. Are you interested in succeeding, flourishing and thriving in every area of your life? You can!

Spirit, Soul and Body

You are a three-part being: You are a spirit, you have a soul and you live in a body (1 Thessalonians 5:23).

Your spirit, when born again by the Spirit of God, is brand new in Christ. Old things have passed away and all things have become new. In Christ, your spirit is complete, perfect and righteous (John

3:3-6; 2 Corinthians 5:17). Eternal life, the kingdom of God and His shekhinah glory dwell within your spirit when you are born again. You are a powerhouse within!

Your body is your physical form. When it is in submission to your born-again spirit, your physical body performs the works of Jesus in the earth. When your body is not in submission to your spirit, it performs the deeds of the flesh.

Your soul hosts your mind, emotions and will. It is the gate-keeper for the life-making decisions you make that affect you for good or for evil. 3 John 1:2 helps us understand that when this part of your being prospers, you can be in health and prosper in other areas of life, too.

Through Jesus, you have already been filled with success, per-fection and glory within your spirit, but in order to have the flow of that life made manifest in your outward life, your soul needs to be in agreement with your spirit.

Can you imagine yourself in vibrant physical, emotional, men-tal and spiritual health, prospering in every area of your life? Do you desire to experience these glorious qualities? You can!

You can tap into God's realm of health and prosperity, where everything in your life flourishes and overflows in abundance. According to 3 John 1:2, this state is largely dependent on the prosperity of your soul (mind, emotions and will). When your soul is prosperous, it attracts vibrant health and prosperity.

What Does a Prosperous Soul Look Like?

A prosperous soul is optimistic, positive and faith-filled – aligned with God's perspective, life, promises and truth. A prosperous soul is free of anxiety, bitterness, offense, anger, doubt, wounding and negativity.

You Attract What You Believe

Jesus said, "Anything is possible if a person believes." Mark 9:23 (NLT) The Law of Attraction responds to the thoughts and emotions you believe – whether positive or negative, true or false. What do you believe?

Medical scientists and practitioners are able to measure brain waves and the frequencies of thoughts. Every thought you have releases frequencies and produces effects in response to The Law of Attraction. How you think and feel is a result of what you believe, and what you believe will be attracted to you.

For example, if you look at yourself in the mirror, gasp at the possibility that you have gained weight and think, "Oh no, I am gaining weight." That thought is what you believe. Many who study quantum physics are concluding that immediately that thought goes out into the universe with frequencies that attract more thoughts like it. Eventually, those thoughts will manifest in the choices you make concerning what you eat or how you take care of your body. The Law of Attraction calls forth the manifestation of what you believe.

The great news is that the Law of Attraction can work for you instead of against you. For example, if you are excited about a job interview because you are confident that you will be favored in the eyes of the employer, you can attract that person's favor.

Much of what you are experiencing in your life right now you have attracted to yourself. You continually attract to yourself that which you believe, whether positive or negative.

The Law of Attraction is not biased. It does not take into consideration whether you want the outcome or not. The Law of Attraction works for all people the same way. It attracts to you the things that you believe in your thoughts and feelings.

Remember the definition of The Law of Attraction:

I attract into my life whatever I give my thoughts, feelings, attention, energy, focus and belief to – whether positive or negative.

Your Beliefs Create Faith or Fear

"Now faith is the substance of things hoped for, the evidence of things not seen." —Hebrews 11:1 (NKJV)

Romans 10:17 teaches that "faith comes from hearing, and hearing by the word of Christ."

The word of Christ is the gospel. It is the good news that Jesus, through His death and resurrection, has made every blessing and promise of God available to us (Ephesians 1:3; 2 Corinthians 1:20). It is the knowledge and understanding of "the grace of our Lord Jesus Christ, that though He was rich, yet for your sake He became poor, so that you through His poverty might become rich." 2 Corinthians 8:9

Continually hearing and believing the word of Christ is what creates faith in our soul to believe God for everything else in life – causing us to be confident that "He who did not spare His own Son, but delivered Him over for us all, how will He not also with Him freely give us all things?" (Romans 8:32)

The original Greek term translated *word* in Romans 10:17, is "rhema." Rhema is the inspired word of God that comes to you by His Spirit. It is not just the print on the page in your Bible. How does rhema come to us? Most of the time it is through faint thoughts and images in our mind's eye. For example, you may read several chapters of Scripture, but suddenly one particular verse jumps out and speaks to you personally.

Rhema is a revelation given into your mind (thoughts and imagination) that releases hope (joyful expectation), and hope can produce faith. When faith is birthed, then that which has entered your mind can begin to manifest. The truth of that Spirit-breathed revelation becomes your internal reality and the substance or manifestation of the promise it carries is attracted to you as you believe it.

If your soul believes God's promises with hope and excitement, positive thoughts go out as frequencies that attract like substance. That which God has spoken to you, mixed with faith, will eventually manifest.

Even unbelievers have a measure of faith. Everyone has the ability to believe and exercise the law of faith, but only God's faith – which enters us at salvation – can be in complete harmony with His ultimate truth and purposes for your life. God is attracted to His faith in you that was birthed through your thoughts and feelings aligned to His will. His faith is the most holy faith (Jude 1:20) and it is always based on His truth and eternal purposes. As your soul prospers in alignment with His truth, ways and purposes, your whole life will prosper.

On the flip side, Job said, "What I fear comes upon me" (Job 3:25). Fear is a negative force birthed by believing negative thoughts. It works the same as faith. That which you fear can come upon you. Fear is like a magnet that can attract to you the very thing you fear. This is another example of The Law of Attraction at work.

When you understand The Law of Attraction, you are able to intentionally partner with God and His purposes for your life to create realms of fulfilled desire and goodness. This is how your soul prospers. God's Law of Attraction was created for you.

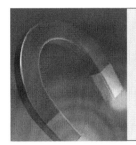

> "As your soul's posture is before God, so goes your life. It is out of your soul with its beliefs and alignment to God's ways and purposes that you create the outcomes of your life."
> —Patricia King

Summary

1. When you think positive thoughts, you attract positive results. When you think negative thoughts you attract negative results.

2. The key verse that reveals God's Law of Attraction is 3 John 1:2 "Beloved, I pray that in all respects you may prosper and be in good health, just as your soul prospers."

3. As your soul (mind, emotions and will) are aligned to God's Word and ways, then you will prosper according to His goodness and intention for your life.

4. The Law of Attraction is not biased. It does not take into consideration whether you want the outcome or not. The Law of Attraction works for all people the same way. It attracts to you the things that you believe in your thoughts and feelings.

5. Much of what you are experiencing in your life right now you attracted to yourself. You continually attract to yourself that which you believe, whether positive or negative.

6. Your beliefs create faith or fear. Fear is negative faith. Both faith and fear attract what you believe.

7. You can intentionally partner with God to create realms of fulfilled desire and goodness in your life.

Activation

1. Think of someone you know who is favored or successful in their life. What do you see that contributes to the favor in their life? Can you see God's Law of Attraction at work? How?

2. Think of someone you know who lives in oppression. What do you see that contributes to the trouble in their life? Can you see God's Law of Attraction at work? How?

Review your own life:

3. What area(s) of your life do you see flourishing? What do you see that contributes to this abundance? Can you see God's Law of Attraction at work? How?

4. What area(s) of your life seem blocked? What do you see that contributes to the blockage? Can you see God's Law of Attraction at work? How?

CHAPTER THREE

Your Prosperous Mind

"The mind focused on success will surely attract it."
—Author Unknown

Your Prosperous Mind

O ver the next few chapters, we'll examine more deeply the three parts of your soul – your mind, emotions and will – and learn how they can begin to prosper according to God's Law of Attraction. Let's start with the mind.

Your Prosperous Mind

A prosperous mind is filled with thoughts, images and meditations on the promises of God and sets its focus on that which is in line with His truth.

> "Finally, brethren, whatever is true, whatever is honorable, whatever is right, whatever is pure, whatever is lovely, whatever is of good repute, if there is any excellence and if anything worthy of praise, dwell on these things... and the God of peace will be with you."   —Philippians 4:8-9b

> "Set your mind on the things above, not on the things that are on earth."   —Colossians 3:2

God is attracted to Himself in you and to His attributes and promises that you meditate on. You attract a heavenly environment filled with love, goodness and power when you think on heavenly things. You are filled with godly character when you meditate on His virtues. You attract the manifestation of God's promises when you fill your mind and imagination with the fulfillment of those promises. This is The Law of Attraction as God purposed it to work.

You are continually attracting something godly or ungodly, depending on what you are thinking about. As we have seen, your overall prosperity is connected to the prosperity of your soul. Your mind, which is part of your soul, prospers when it dwells on the goodness of God, His promises and His truth.

Negative and ungodly thoughts work the same way, but they attract negative and ungodly effects – whether you desire them to or not. It is important to watch over your thoughts. Always keep them aligned with God's truth and resist things that are contrary to His Word. The Law of Attraction does not distinguish between our good and bad thoughts. You can attract things that you don't want just as easily as you attract things that you desire. What you attract depends on what dominates your thoughts.

Fill Your Mind with God-Thoughts

"For as he thinks in his heart, so is he."
—Proverbs 23:7a (NKJV)

Years ago, I wrote a book containing decrees from the Word of God that you can proclaim into various areas of your life. *Decrees* is available at XPministries.com, and I have also included a bonus copy for you at the back of this book. I regularly read these decrees out loud, or sometimes I read them silently and ponder each statement, allowing the meditation of their truth to fill my mind.

At times, I will choose one decree (such as the decree for wisdom, provision, godly character, favor or blessing) and focus on it for an entire week or longer. Every day, I will meditate on each line and proclaim it over and over until it is firmly established in my thoughts.

I have also recorded the *Decree* book in audio format with music in the background, so I can soak in the decrees while engaged in other activities. I use this tool while prayer walking, cleaning the house or engaging in mundane activities. It gives my mind an opportunity to be filled with the truth of God's Word even when I am engaged in other things that absorb my attention.

There are many such print and audio tools available – books, audio Bibles, soaking CDs, etc. – that can help you saturate your mind with God's truth and promises.

This constant focus of the mind is called meditation. To meditate simply means to focus one's thoughts on something. Biblical meditation involves reflecting on, pondering over, muttering and speaking under your breath God's truth. Remember that you attract that which fills your mind. Look at what the Scriptures promise to those who meditate on God's Word:

"How blessed is the man who does not walk in the counsel of the wicked, nor stand in the path of sinners, nor sit in the seat of scoffers! But his delight is in the law of the Lord, and in His law he meditates day and night. He will be like a tree firmly planted by streams of water, which yields its fruit in its season and its leaf does not wither; and in whatever he does, he prospers."   —Psalm 1:1-3

Meditation on the Word of God creates prosperity in your soul – and when your soul prospers, everything else prospers!

The Bible teaches us to renew our mind (Romans 12:2). Your mind is always absorbing something – consciously or subconsciously. There are many sounds transmitted in the atmosphere around you that your mind receives without your awareness. Some of those sounds are positive and life-giving, while others are negative, vain and destructive. Protect what you submit your mind to as much as possible by intentionally filling it with that which is true, lovely and of good report. Positive, life-giving words will cancel negative words and their effect on your life. Keep your mind renewed by aligning it with God's promises found in His Word.

Your Imagination

Another part of your mind is your imagination. It is through your imagination that you receive impressions, images and vision. God is a visionary God and He made you in His image and likeness. You have vision all the time, but you may not be aware of it. Your mind thinks in pictures – that's vision.

Your thoughts produce images in your imagination. For example, if I said to you, "I have a dog named Big Bruno," immediately you are picturing a dog in your mind's eye, because words produce images. If I then said, "Come, let me introduce you to Big Bruno," and proceeded to pick up a soft, fluffy white animal that purred and uttered a meow, you would be confused. Why? Because I told you I had a dog, not a cat. Your mind's eye saw a dog, so when I showed you a cat, there was confusion.

Similarly, if I introduced you to Big Bruno and he happened to be a one-and-a-half pound Chihuahua, you would be equally surprised. Why? Because you probably imagined a larger dog, like a Labrador or Saint Bernard. You are always seeing images or impressions in your mind's eye (imagination), but you may not be consciously aware of them.

Have you ever had a friend tell you about someone they know and when you were finally introduced to them, you were shocked? That's because you pictured them a certain way in your mind's eye based on your friend's description. We think with images. Our thoughts and our imagination are connected to each other as part of the mind. What you think on, you imagine and what you imagine, you think on.

Bible meditation involves the use of the imagination, too. That is why God filled the Scriptures with visions and stories for you to enjoy. He knows that if you can see it, you can have it.

Successful business leaders understand the power of meditating on thoughts and images that promote success. They will reflect throughout the day on closing deals or succeeding in a particular assignment or product sale. Many also create vision boards for their executive and sales teams, because they know the power of images to produce thoughts that ultimately attract results.

I have a prayer album that I made. It's full of images and Scriptures that I have collected and taped into a three-ring binder. As I pray, I look at the images because they connect me to what I am believing for. Throughout the day those images flash into my mind and help keep me focused on my prayer project. I have also enjoyed the creative process of making the prayer binder. I highly recommend it.

God's Vision Board

God took Abraham out on the plains and asked him to look at the stars in the sky in order to deliver a promise to him.

> "And He took him outside and said, 'Now look toward the heavens, and count the stars, if you are able to count them.' And He said to him, 'So shall your descendants be.'"
>
> —Genesis 15:5

I am sure that every night, as Abraham gazed at the stars, he was reminded of God's promise. God created a "vision board" for Abraham so that Abraham's imagination could be fixed on the promise of God. Abraham's soul, filled with vision of the promise, would go on to prosper and attract the blessing.

What pictures fill your mind? The prosperous soul sees the way God sees and agrees with His purposes – on earth as it is in heaven. The prosperous mind sees success, goodness and blessing. When you can see it, you can have it. What do you see?

Jesus said that He only did the things He saw His Father do (John 5:19). He filled His soul (imagination) with visions of the Father's will and then performed what He saw.

A woman recently asked me to pray for a cancerous growth she was fighting in her body. When she initially asked me to minister to her, I did not have assurance of faith for the miracle in my heart, even though I knew God could do it. I did not want to pray without the assurance, so I silently asked the Lord to show me the healing.

As I waited, I saw a faint vision in my mind's eye of His hand touching the growth and it disappeared. I continued to quietly reflect and focus on the impression until it got stronger and more defined in my mind's eye. The more I meditated on the vision, the more my faith grew until I had full assurance and confidence to pray.

I then did what I saw in the vision. In Jesus' name, I laid my hand on the growth and declared her healed. The growth disappeared immediately. It was a miracle of healing just as I had seen in my imagination. The image in my mind was imparted and cultivated by the Holy Spirit.

You will prosper and be in health as your soul prospers. Your imagination is part of your soul and when it is submitted to God's perspective and will, you will attract what you see.

Negative Images

Remember, you attract what you see. When negative imaginations that are contrary to God's promises for you come into your mind, immediately cast them down and replace them with God-images.

The apostle Paul taught the church at Corinth to cast down imaginations that were contrary to the knowledge of God. We should do the same and only allow our minds to be filled with blessed God-thoughts and images.

"Casting down imaginations, and every high thing that exalteth itself against the knowledge of God, and bringing into captivity every thought to the obedience of Christ."

—2 Corinthians 10:5 (KJV)

The Invitation

God is inviting you to cleanse your mind from everything that is negative and non-productive and intentionally fill it with good things. He came to give you life in all its goodness and abundance (John 10:10). When your soul is filled with thoughts, images and meditations that are in accordance with His goodness, grace and love, they will manifest in your life. This is God's Law of Attraction.

"When your thoughts, imaginations and feelings are focused on God's goodness, promises, love and truth, you will have a prosperous soul. It is then that everything else in life can prosper."
—Patricia King

Summary

1. Your mind includes your thoughts and imagination.

2. A prosperous mind is filled with thoughts, images and meditations on the promises of God and sets its focus on that which is in line with His truth.

3. Through Scripture, we are taught to set our mind on things that are good, heavenly and positive (Philippians 4:8, Colossians 3:2).

4. You are continually attracting something, godly or ungodly, depending on what you are thinking about.

5. The focus of the mind's pondering is called meditation. Scripture confirms the blessings of success, prosperity,

fruitfulness and vibrancy that come from meditating on the Word of God (Psalm 1:1-3).

6. Your mind is always absorbing something – consciously or subconsciously.

7. The Bible teaches us to renew our mind (Romans 12:2). Tools such as written and audio decrees of the Word of God, audio Bibles, soaking CDs, etc. can help you renew your mind.

8. You receive impressions, images and vision through your imagination.

9. God is a visionary God and He made you in His image and likeness. Your mind thinks in pictures.

10. You have vision all the time but you may not be aware of it.

11. The Law of Attraction works according to what you envision.

12. Positive images in your mind that are aligned with God's truth and fill your soul with joy and expectation will attract life and blessing to you.

13. Negative images will attract oppression and calamity.

14. Scripture teaches us to cast down negative thoughts that are contrary to God's will and turn them around to be obedient to God's promises (2 Corinthians 10:5).

15. God is inviting you to cleanse your mind from everything that is negative and non-productive and intentionally fill it with good things.

16. When your soul is filled with thoughts, images and meditations that are in accordance with His goodness, grace and love, they will manifest in your life. This is God's Law of Attraction.

Activation

1. Make a list of the things you are fearful, worried or anxious about. Go through each one and ask the Lord to reveal His wonderful, intended will, plans and outcomes for you in those areas. Write down what He reveals through thoughts, images and Scriptures.

2. Take one of the items on your list and take time to intentionally cast down all negative and fearful thoughts about it and replace them with God's.

3. Dream and envision in your mind the wonderful outcome when God's plan is realized. Write it in a journal with details of what you see and think. Speak out what you are seeing.

4. Determine to only believe and see what the Lord has revealed. If a negative or fearful thought returns, cast it down and replace it.

5. Meditate every day on the wonderful outcome you see. Remind yourself throughout the day.

6. Record the testimony of the manifestation of God's Law of Attraction. It will build your faith for the next one.

7. Repeat steps 2-6 for every other point on your list.

CHAPTER FOUR

Your Prosperous Emotions

"A person who lacks control over their emotions is in danger of sabotaging the fulfillment of their destiny."

—Patricia King

Your Prosperous Emotions

Your thoughts, visions and perceptions produce feelings or emotions that are also part of your soul. For example, if you were to think about a fun memory from your past, it might produce a light and happy feeling. If you were to imagine getting a raise at work, you might feel expectant or excited.

On the other hand, if you were to think about a thief breaking into your home, you could experience feelings of fear, anxiety or terror. That is because your thoughts produce feelings. If you have feelings, there are thoughts behind them – whether you are aware of them or not. Feelings or emotions are part of your soul's function.

How you feel about things produces a manifestation of what those feelings represent. Remember what it says in the book of Job, "What I fear comes upon me" (Job 3:25).

It is not enough to simply have mental agreement toward a promise in God's Word. For example, I might agree in my mind that God can cause a person to come out of their wheelchair and walk, but when I look at them in the chair and my mind is challenged by what I see, it produces feelings that are full of doubt. I am more likely to believe my feelings in that moment than a foundational doctrinal truth that I know in my mind. It is because my mind became doubtful and anxious and my emotions reinforced that belief. What you feel wields a powerful influence on what you believe.

I know of many people who generally believe that God is good, and yet they do not see God's goodness manifesting in their life. They will tell me, "I don't feel His love and acceptance for me," or "I feel God is passing me by." As a result, they doubt that He is near them or that He loves them and desires to show them His goodness. Somewhere behind that feeling is a thought. This person agrees with the Bible and believes that God is good. But there is also a belief in them that might think, "But maybe He doesn't want to show me goodness because I am not worthy." This individual has two competing thoughts. The one that generates a feeling trumps the one that doesn't. Your feelings will reveal and reinforce your predominant thoughts and beliefs.

Your feelings or senses are important because when they are rightly aligned with God's truth, they will produce prosperity in your soul that will attract to yourself what you are feeling.

Many scriptures speak about the heart. Sometimes this refers to your spirit, but oftentimes in the Bible, "heart" is another word used for your soul. The heart (your emotions, feelings, thoughts, imagination and will) needs to be cared for and nurtured so that you can live in prosperity and health.

"Watch over your heart with all diligence, for from it flow the springs of life."   —Proverbs 4:23

First Impressions Form Powerful Feelings

Your first response to something can set a lasting tone. Leaders in the business world are aware that first impressions are important. They are aware that it is important for a person to have a good initial "feeling" in order for their product or business to be accepted.

For example, you might go into a restaurant that makes the best chicken dinner in town, but if you are rudely treated at the door, you might not stay for dinner. Even if you do, the initial treatment you received will produce a bad feeling that you will likely remember more than how great the chicken tasted. Whenever someone mentions the name of that restaurant, you will recall the bad feeling you had and you probably won't desire to visit that restaurant again.

I remember once ordering breakfast at a restaurant. When I ate the first bite of the egg, it tasted "fishy." It turned my stomach and I spit out the egg on the plate. My entire body felt distressed and repulsed. I have never again gone into that restaurant chain. Every time I see one of that chain's restaurants, my emotional memory kicks in and I drive right by.

In our ministry, when we are serving the Lord's people, whether it is in a conference, church service, television program or evangelism on the streets, I encourage our team to create a good first experience for the people. The feeling they initially have will attract more of the same throughout the event or encounter. That initial good feeling will open their hearts to receive the Word of God that will transform their lives.

Sports Psychology

Athletes are trained in physical development, but they also spend a great deal of time getting their thoughts aligned with the mind of a champion. They understand that their thoughts produce feelings and that in order to be a champion, they need to feel like a champion.

I recently met a sports psychologist who shared how the brain responds to physical movements that create feelings. She led me in a series of body movements used by champions. As a result, I became filled with feelings of strength and victory. These deliberate physical movements relayed messages to my brain that I was a champion and those thoughts, in turn, produced the feelings of a champion.

Emotions in the Bible

The Scriptures speak a lot about emotions – even God has them. One example is found in Psalm 2:1-4, where the kings of the earth are coming against God's anointed, yet God's emotional response is to laugh. God is not worried or anxious. His emotions are congruent with His truth.

David is another example of emotions in the Bible. In one instance, when David and his men went into Ziklag after the Amalekites had burned it down and taken their women and children captive, it says that "David and his men wept aloud until they had no strength left to weep." 1 Samuel 30:4 (NIV)

David and his men were feeling greatly distressed over their horrific loss. In verse 6, it describes a further terrible situation for David. The people were so embittered against him that they wanted to stone him. David felt discouraged, but instead of allowing his soul (feelings) to remain in despair, the Scripture says that, "David strengthened himself in the Lord his God" (1 Samuel 30:6b).

David turned his feelings around and chose strength in the Lord over discouragement. He chose to remember who he was – a covenant child of God, the head and not the tail, above and not beneath (Deuteronomy 28:13). Instead of allowing his feelings to be controlled by his circumstances, David went to God for strength.

In Psalm 103, we get a glimpse into how David would strengthen his soul in times like these. He would speak to it! He would say things like, "Bless the Lord, O my soul, and all that is within me, bless His holy name. Bless the Lord, O my soul, and forget none of His benefits" (Psalm 103:1-2). David commanded his soul to focus on blessing the Lord and remembering all the good benefits God had promised him.

Every time I focus intentionally on blessing the Lord by thinking and speaking of His goodness, my feelings are affected. Joy fills my heart and the joy of the Lord becomes my strength.

In the midst of the horrific disaster at Ziklag, David chose to strengthen his soul in the Lord. As he did, the word of the Lord came to him: "Pursue, for you shall surely overtake them and without fail recover all." 1 Samuel 30:8 (AMP) He did pursue. He did overtake and he did recover all.

The prosperity of that victory began with a change of heart (feeling). If David had remained in depression and remorse, he may not have been able to receive the strength of the Lord and the word of direction that transformed that devastating situation into a great triumph.

God's Law of Attraction was at work in David's life. He chose to fill his soul with God-thoughts and feelings, focusing on His goodness. When David's soul was aligned, the word of the Lord was attracted to him. When he believed and acted on the word, the victory was made manifest.

Don't Let Your Emotions Control Your Life

Until I was about thirty years of age, I wore my emotions on my sleeve. I allowed my emotions to control my life. Before coming to Christ, I would always lean into my feelings and as a result, I attracted a lot of unwanted outcomes. I had to learn to take dominion over my emotions, making them align with God's Word. The Holy Spirit taught me to speak to my soul just like David did and to bring my emotions into line with the truth. As I learned to do that, I attracted manifestations of the promises of God. Watch over your soul with all diligence!

As mentioned earlier, behind your feelings are thoughts and beliefs. Therefore, if you are feeling that you are not loved by God, for example, there are ungodly thoughts and beliefs behind that emotion. Find those thoughts and turn them around. Replace the negative thoughts with God's truth and demand that your feelings respond to God's truth. Meditate on His truth until your feelings change.

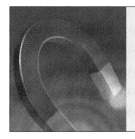

"Disappointment is inevitable. But to become discouraged, it is a choice I make. God is the God of all encouragement."

—*Charles Stanley*

Practice Walking with God in the Mundane Things of Life

God can teach you His wisdom even in the simple, little, mundane things of life. I had fun practicing the dynamics of The Law of Attraction with my husband, Ron, in an enjoyable game that we sometimes played together. For years, I could seldom win this game. I felt very subtly, and somewhat unconsciously, that Ron would always win and I would lose, so I did lose – almost every time. I attracted loss. The Law of Attraction was at work.

When I was being taught by God how His Law of Attraction works, for fun I put it into practice when playing this game with my husband. Before I played, I would meditate on the Scripture: "I am more than a conqueror" (Romans 8:37). I chose to believe that I was "the head and not the tail; above and not beneath" (Deuteronomy 28:13).

I started to imagine myself winning. I allowed the reality and the peace of God's goodness to fill me until I felt like a winner. Joy started to fill me emotionally at the thought of winning. When I played the game, I delighted in the Lord's favor and... I won every round.

Whenever a round was looking disastrous, I would think to myself, "I am a winner, so even though this doesn't look like it is in my favor, it is. This game favors me." As I thought of being a winner, I felt joy within. By the end of the round, I had won. (Ha, ha – yes, you can apply the Scripture to every area of your life! God cares about every facet of it.)

Ron would say things like, "I just can't win" or "you always get the breaks." I would silently agree within myself with a smile, "yes, that is right." Throughout the game, I would continue to ponder – out of rest, not anxiety or pressure (this is important) – the fact that I was a winner. The inner sense or feeling of being a winner filled me and I held onto that and protected it even when contrary thoughts and feelings attempted to enter.

After a number of times of playing the game with notable results, I shared my "secret" with Ron. At first he was a bit skeptical, but I kept winning and he kept complaining that he was losing. I shared with him again about God's Law of Attraction and then he caught it. He won the next round and the next. I laughed. It made me happy to see him "get it." I was a winner whether the game was won by me, my husband or by anyone else. I did not let a loss change the fact that I was a winner at my core. I was anchored in my soul as a winner and refused to change my perspective or my feeling. It was settled in quietness, confidence and rest within. I had a prosperous soul and it showed.

This is perhaps a silly, humdrum example, but the exercise of meditating on the truth that, in Christ, I am a winner and that He has called me to triumph in Him (2 Corinthians 2:14), established in me a strong core focus for other more important areas of my life. If we are faithful in the little things we encounter each day, we will flourish in the more important things in life, too. We need to practice aligning our thoughts and feelings with God's Word in every situation in life.

As mentioned before, most people believe what they feel over what they think. You could think, "I am a winner," but if you feel like a loser, you will probably believe that you are a loser. What you feel is more important than what you think because that is what is more believable to you most of the time. However, what you think produces your feelings, so both your thoughts and feelings need to be established in God's truth.

No Anxious Striving

When learning how to align your soul with God's will, do not get anxious or strive within yourself. When you lose your peace, you lose your focus. Your prosperity of soul requires healthy, joyful determination from a place of inner rest and peace.

For example, if you do not "feel" God's love, do not strive to feel it. First of all, in peace, intentionally choose to believe the truth about His love with healthy, joyful determination, whether you feel it or not. Meditate on the truth of His love in quietness of soul. Again, I emphasize, it is important not to be anxious or stressed. Be at peace in rest of soul. Eventually, you will begin to feel and sense His love. Once you have your initial breakthrough, increase will come. God's presence is attracted to what you believe and focus on in your mind, imagination and emotions.

To help you grow in the revelation of God's love for you, I highly recommend a soaking CD entitled *Ultimate Passion*, listed at the back of this book. It will fill your mind with the truth about God's love for you, which, in turn, will help you feel His love.

You Can Determine Your Feelings

If you discover that you are having negative, fearful or hurtful feelings, you have the power to change them. You do not need to let your emotions control you. You can control your emotions.

Once, I was hurt by a friend and my emotions were affected. I felt the hurt. I took time to forgive my friend from my heart. Then, I began to meditate on how safe I was in God's love and how He was strengthening me. I saw an image in my mind's eye of Jesus carrying my grief and sorrow away. I saw Him healing my wounded soul. The more I meditated on the thoughts and images I was receiving, the more the emotion lifted and even changed to that of hope and strength. Over the next week, whenever the hurt feeling would return, I would once again saturate my thoughts in those God-given meditations. I made a demand on my emotions to come into line with the truth – and they did.

Your emotions attract what you are feeling. God's Law of Attraction responds to your emotions. People who feel depressed attract more depression. People who feel successful attract more success. What do you want to attract? Determine your feelings, determine the outcome.

"Feelings and emotions are beautiful. The ability to emote was created in us so that we might know and experience the pleasure and goodness of God."   —Patricia King

Summary

1. Your feelings produce the manifestation of what they represent.

2. Your thoughts produce feelings.

3. God has feelings and you were created in His image and likeness.

4. When you change your thoughts, you can change your feelings.

5. Your first impression of something produces feelings.

6. Athletes know the importance of feeling like a champion if they are going to win.

7. When you are addressing your feelings, do not be anxious. Be determined in rest, peace and joy.

8. You can determine your feelings.

Activation

1. Choose something delightful – a dream or vision that you would like to see manifest in your life – and write it out with as much detail as you can.

2. Ask the Lord to confirm His agreement with this dream or desire. Wait on Him. He will speak to you in your thoughts and will often confirm it through Bible verses. Write down what He shows you.

Learning to Hear God's Voice is a wonderful audio teaching that will help you hear His voice. It is listed under the resource section at the back of the book.

3. Identify your feelings when you think about this desire being fulfilled. Write down what you are feeling.

4. If you identify any negative or fearful emotions, ask the Lord to reveal the thought(s) behind them and then address those thoughts until your emotions are settled in God's truth.

5. Throughout the week, intentionally ponder your dream and let your emotions fill with anticipation for its fulfillment.

CHAPTER FIVE

Your Prosperous Will

"Destiny is no matter of chance. It is a matter of choice. It is not a thing to be waited for, it is a thing to be achieved."

—William Jennings Bryan

Your Prosperous Will

The third part of your soul is your will. In order for your soul to prosper, your will needs to come into agreement with God's truth and goodness. If you want to prosper, you must choose prosperous results. Your will is the gatekeeper – with it you choose good or evil, right or wrong, prosperity or poverty.

You choose what you receive into your heart – sometimes without even realizing it. For example, I was having dinner with some elderly people one evening. One of them said, "When we get older all we talk about is our aches and pains." I injected a positive testimony into the conversation and said, "I praise the Lord that I do not have one ache or pain." One of the ladies responded jokingly, "Well, you can have some of mine. I will gladly give you a few."

I knew she was joking, and the rest of the guests were laughing. If my guard had not been up, I could have simply laughed along. However, I understood that if I came into agreement with her, even if it was not a serious belief in my mind, The Law of Attraction could begin to open the gate of my life to receiving her aches and pains.

Instead, both my husband and I said, in the same breath, "No!" We intentionally – with our wills – rejected the invitation. We laughed as we said it, so that she would not feel embarrassed, but we explained, "We do not want to receive any aches and pains. We accept only God's strength and health." Our will was choosing what we would allow into our lives.

Discern the Will of God

Your will is to be aligned with God's will. You are to allow His purposes and truth into your life and reject those things that are not congruent with them. Your will is the gatekeeper.

> "Your kingdom come. Your will be done, on earth as it is in heaven."   —Matthew 6:10

God's will is His purpose. It is His desire. Discern God's will and align your will to it. For example, we have seen that it is God's will for us to prosper. When you align our will in agreement with His, God's Law of Attraction is activated. It is equally important that you come out of alignment and agreement with those things that are not God's will.

One morning over coffee, a ministry friend shared with me a very negative prophetic word that had been given to her by a spiritual leader in a city where she had ministered. I was alarmed. It was clearly a curse and not a word from God at all. The true New Testament prophetic word edifies, exhorts and comforts. This word condemned and cursed, but it had come so quickly and unexpectedly that it had caught my friend off guard. She was jolted by the word and it entered her heart, producing fear. As she processed it later, she realized in her thoughts that it was not from God, and yet she had continued to be tormented with fear and uncertainty about her calling for months.

That morning, I took dominion over that curse in Jesus' name. I decreed, "This was not a word from God, it was from the enemy!" I invited my friend to choose to cast the word out of her soul. She did so and was set free. Any time the words of that false prophecy would come back to her mind, she would choose again to cast them down and replace them with God's truth about herself.

Your will is the gatekeeper to your soul. You choose what you accept and what you reject. Watch over your heart with all diligence so that it is full of God's ways, plans, truth and glorious eternal realities.

> "I call heaven and earth to witness against you today, that I have set before you life and death, the blessing and the curse. So choose life in order that you may live, you and your descendants."   —Deuteronomy 30:19

Choose with your will to fill your mind, imagination and emotions only with God's goodness and truth. If you do so, your soul will prosper, and if your soul prospers you will prosper in life and be in health.

Determination

Your will also speaks of determination. You might hear someone say, "I willed myself to win the race." That means they determined with their will to do what it took to win that race. Athletes often feel weak towards the end of a race. Their body feels pain and they have no energy left. Nevertheless, they will stir up their will and determine to finish. They will to fight off the thoughts that say, "I can't do it, I can't finish." Instead they say, "I can do it. I can finish. I can do it." They are exercising their will to finish and to win. As a result, God's Law of Attraction goes to work and attracts strength to finish the race.

I was helping a couple once with a financial hurdle they were facing. They had gotten into enormous debt and creditors were knocking at their door. They were overwhelmed by their situation. Getting out of debt looked impossible to them, so they didn't bother making payments. They thought, "We can't pay it off so why try." They were very discouraged and had been in a slump for a few years. Their negative thoughts and emotions were attracting even more debt. They were trapped in a mindset of lack.

I gave them a good pep talk and encouraged them to go for it. I assured them that their debt could be paid off and that they could build with God to carve out a realm of prosperity in their lives. That evening, they willed to make a quality decision to move forward and remove every obstacle to their prosperity.

We prayed and believed their debt would be removed and put a plan together to pay it off. We put a three-year goal into place, but I assured them that once they came into agreement with God's promises and acted with integrity to pay off their debt, things would shift and they could possibly have everything paid off much sooner. God's Law of Attraction would go to work on their behalf.

That couple purposed with everything they had to pay off their debts. They focused on it with joy and made sacrifices to make extra payments. They trimmed expenses every place they could and applied those funds toward their debt. Extra employment opportunities opened up once in a while and some unexpected sources of income showed up in the process. God also gave them creative ideas, like hosting garage and bake sales, to make extra funds to apply toward the loans. It was sometimes only a few extra dollars here and there, but through their determined effort, in less than 18 months all their debt was paid off and they were able to start fulfilling other desires.

God's Law of Attraction worked on their behalf to attract a realm of debt-free living that they are still living in today. They chose to start living within their means and believing God for the increase. Their determination paid off! They started seeing themselves in abundance rather than in lack. They chose to believe God's promises and activate His wisdom. Today, they live in abundance. Abundance is now attracted to them as they live debt-free.

Your will is powerful. Sometimes you have to fight through resistance in your thoughts and feelings with sheer determination. A woman I knew was once so discouraged and depressed over her singleness that she had chosen to abandon all hope of ever finding a good husband. She simply complained about her singleness. Guess what she attracted? More years of singleness. That woman had been so afraid of being disappointed if she dared to hope, that she had remained single. Sad. I encouraged her to use her will to push through the discouragement and to lay hold of her desire. I have seen many men and women in their later years overcome fear and discouragement to find their mate.

Your will is indeed powerful and it is part of your soul. When you align your will with God's purposes and pleasure, you will prosper as your soul prospers.

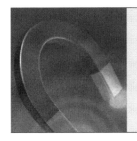

"We are not victims of circumstances that appear to be overpowering. We have the power of choice. Choose to be an overcomer."
—Patricia King

Summary

1. The third part of your soul is your will. If you want to prosper, you must choose prosperous results.

2. Discern the will of God and come into agreement with it. When your will aligns with His, you prosper.

3. Your will is the gatekeeper to your soul. You choose what you accept and what you reject. Watch over your heart with all diligence so that it is full of God's ways, plans, truth and glorious eternal realities.

4. Your will is powerful. Sometimes you have to fight through resistance in your thoughts and feelings with sheer determination.

Activation

1. Think of one unfulfilled desire that you have in your life. Ask yourself if you are choosing to come into complete agreement with God and His promises in that area by casting down every thought that is contrary to it. If not, take note and take action.

2. Choose to press in. Choose to meditate on the breakthrough. Choose to lay hold of a vision of victory.

CHAPTER SIX

Your Prosperous Health

"God wants you well. God wants you prosperous. God wants you a whole person."
                                        —Oral Roberts

Your Prosperous Health

Today, people are becoming more interested in health and wellness. Individuals, corporations and even governments are promoting healthier lifestyles. This is a good thing. More focus on health will result in less need for healing.

Health is different from healing. You need healing when you are sick or injured, but health is the glorious state of vibrancy in spirit, soul and body that God wants us to live in all the time. In heaven there is absolute health. Jesus invites us to live on earth as it is in heaven.

Health in Your Spirit

As mentioned earlier, you are a three-part being. You are a spirit, you have a soul, and you live in a body. When you are born again of the Spirit of God, your spirit has been made new – old things have passed away. Your born-again spirit has no sin, sickness, disease or injury. It has no demonization or brokenness. Your spirit has the very life of Christ in it, the fullness of His light has expelled all darkness. Everything of Christ now dwells within you. He gives you His eternal life, nature, character, strength, gifts, abilities and health. This cannot be earned – it is a gift. Your born-again spirit is your holy of holies. The glory of God dwells within you. You have perfect health within your inner self.

Health in Your Soul

Your mental and emotional health is important for vibrant living. Your soul, when aligned to God's truth, will cause you to prosper (flourish, succeed and overflow in every area of your life). The condition of your soul determines your outcomes in life – for good or for evil. Therefore, it is important to give attention to the health of your soul.

Ten Defining Characteristics of a Healthy Soul

The healthy soul:

1. Is aligned with God's Word, ways and purposes.

2. Is free from sin and receives forgiveness through the blood of Christ.

3. Is free from unforgiveness, bitterness and offense.

4. Chooses love and walks in love.

5. Receives God's peace and is filled with well-being.

6. Believes that every battle in life will produce a victory when focused on the Lord and His promises.

7. Believes God's Word and promises over adverse circumstances in life.

8. Knows that God works everything together for good.

9. Believes the best.

10. Thinks on those things that are good, lovely and of good report.

For your soul to be healthy, your will must choose God's truth over feelings, thoughts, imaginations and circumstances that are contrary to His. When your soul is in health, your physical body will be influenced also.

Ten Practices that Will Help Keep Your Soul in Vibrant Health

1. Read the Word of God and meditate on His promises.

2. Develop an intimate devotional life with the Lord, listening to His voice.

3. Repent immediately and receive forgiveness from any sin – thought, word or deed – so that your heart remains pure.

4. Praise and worship God often. When you focus on Him, His blessings, peace and grace are poured out upon you.

5. Choose relationships that uplift you.

6. Keep short accounts of wrongs, choosing love and forgiveness when hurt.

7. Guard what you submit your soul to, including what type

of music you listen to and movies you watch. Keep clutter out of your mind.

8. Cast down thoughts and imaginations that are raised up against the knowledge of God.

9. Think on things that are good, uplifting, and bring you joy. In the presence of the Lord is fullness of joy. The joy of the Lord is your strength. When your soul is filled with joy, then you will experience health.

10. When in crisis, focus only on God's victory.

Health in Your Body

When you understand the power of the life of God that has filled your spirit, and your soul is in agreement, then your physical body can be quickened with divine health.

"But if the Spirit of Him who raised Jesus from the dead dwells in you, He who raised Christ Jesus from the dead will also give life to your mortal bodies through His Spirit who dwells in you."   —Romans 8:11

When your mind changes to support, agree with and cleave to the truth of God's Word concerning your body, your biology will be affected. God's Law of Attraction will draw to you what you believe. The Spirit of God indwells your human spirit when you are born again. His Spirit within you will give life, energy and empowerment to your mortal body.

People have lost weight, regained energy, experienced strength, healing and supernatural rejuvenation through focusing on God's promises of divine health. Your thoughts concerning yourself and your health can either destroy or build up your body. Remember, The Law of Attraction is impartial. It will attract good or evil, depending on what your soul aligns to.

Sow into Your Health

If we were to spend more time intentionally sowing into our health, we would not deal with sickness and infirmity as much. There are many things you can do to promote good health in your body. In my program, *Power Weight Loss and Rejuvenation*, I teach on five elements needed to promote and maintain vibrant physical health:

1. Nutrition

2. Water

3. Fresh air and sunshine

4. Exercise

5. Detoxing

Even though the program is focused on physical health, I also include devotionals to align your thoughts, vision and beliefs to God's truth. I invest much attention to those aspects, because your physical health is so dependent upon your soul's alignment to God's Word and His ways.

You can take quality vitamins and nutritional supplements, join the gym, bask in the fresh air and sunshine, drink quality water and detox regularly, but if your soul is not aligned, it will not profit you much.

When you invest into vibrant physical health and strength, you will see the results, but your soul's prosperity is very important in this process. Begin to fill your mind (soul) with thoughts of vibrant health. See yourself full of energy and joy. Let your mind think on those things.

Your Mind Controls Your Body

Your mind controls your body. For example, I woke up one day feeling tired. I said to my husband, "I feel so tired and zapped of energy. I don't know how I am going to fulfill my schedule today feeling like this." He responded, "Then you won't." Hey, I wanted a cuddle and some compassion, but I understood immediately what he was communicating.

I made a choice at that moment to bring my confession and my feelings in line with the will of God. I declared boldly, "As my days are, so shall my strength be. God gives strength to the weary." I said it. I sang it. I filled my mind with it, and before long I was strengthened and enjoying physical health and vibrancy.

God's Law of Attraction went to work for me. If I had chosen to think on the negative and focus on my weakness, I would have empowered it. The Law of Attraction would still be at work, drawing to me instead, the life-sapping outcome of what I was thinking, feeling and saying. This Law does not discriminate. It just works, so watch over your heart (soul) with all diligence.

Remember that you will prosper and be in health as your soul prospers. Fill your soul with God' will and purpose and you will live a vibrant and energized life on the earth.

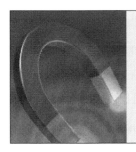
"The Law of Attraction responds to that which flows from your soul. When your soul is aligned with God's truth, you will truly prosper and be in health."
—Patricia King

Summary

1. Health is different from healing. You need healing when you are sick or injured, but health is the glorious state of vibrancy in spirit, soul, and body that God wants us to live in all the time.

2. Health begins in your spirit. When you are born again you receive perfect health in your spirit.

3. A healthy soul (mental and emotional) is important for physical health.

4. The condition of your soul determines your outcomes in life – for good or for evil. Therefore, it is important to give attention to the health of your soul.

5. A healthy soul is free from unforgiveness, bitterness, and offense.

6. When your soul is focused on God's truth, it will be in health and influence your physical body.

Activation

1. Invite the Holy Spirit to reveal to you any area where you have unforgiveness, bitterness or offense. Repent and ask forgiveness.

2. Meditate on God's promises for you to be in health.

3. Envision yourself in perfect health, energized and strengthened.

4. Make word confessions that support divine health in your spirit, soul, and body.

5. Cast down any thoughts that are contrary to God's divine health in you.

6. Intentionally activate The Law of Attraction with regard to your health, and mark the results.

CHAPTER SEVEN

Your Prosperous Relationships

"You are influenced by the company you keep, therefore keep good company." —Patricia King

Your Prosperous Relationships

As we have seen, you are a three-part being: spirit, soul, and body. Your spirit relates to the spiritual realm, your body relates to the physical realm, and your soul relates to the relational realm. You cannot have relationship with God or people without involving your soul. Relationships are interactions between minds, emotions, and wills.

God's Law of Attraction works in relationships, too. You attract people with common interests, values, beliefs, and goals into your life. If you examine any relationship you have, you will find many attributes that attracted you to that relationship. This is important to note, because you become like the company you keep. Whatever you fill your mind and emotions with and set your will to, attracts like substance.

For example, a teenager who listens to music with lyrics that are hateful, sexual and filled with references to drugs will attract others who listen to that same type of music. Music and lyrics are powerful. They infuse the soul with thoughts, imaginations and feelings.

What you meditate on, you attract – and music is a form of meditation. Eventually those teenagers are likely to attract hate, sexual promiscuity and drugs, even if it was not their original intention to participate in those practices. After all, they were "just listening to music." The Law of Attraction is at work.

Relationships accelerate The Law of Attraction. The more relationships you have with others who share the same interests and beliefs as you do, the stronger and quicker the effect of The Law of Attraction is in those areas of your life.

God's Law of Attraction can work powerfully when you connect with healthy relationships. For example, let's say that you love serving the Lord in the area of a healing ministry. As you study the healing gift, healing scriptures, and attend healing lectures, you will find yourself surrounded by others who are of like mind.

Those with common interests speak passionately about those areas, with words that stir, awaken and empower your thoughts, images and feelings. They also invite words to be spoken by you, as you dialogue with them. The synergy produced will attract increased anointing, opportunities and more relationships in that field of interest and endeavor. As you begin to fellowship with these new friends, healing anointing will increase in your life and theirs. The Law of Attraction is intensified in the context of relationships.

As we have seen, The Law of Attraction works just as powerfully in the negative. I once spoke with a heroin addict about his addiction. He shared something that I have never forgotten. "I can go anywhere, in any venue, any city, among any class of people and find the drugs I need," he confided. I asked him how. He said, "It is hard to explain, but basically all you have to do is hang out and those of like nature will be drawn to you. It always works like this. We find each other without a word." That is The Law of Attraction at work.

In corporations, executives will intentionally look for managers with specific character traits, skills and motivations, because they know that if they get the right manager, they will attract others of like traits. That is one of the reasons the interview process in many successful, high-end companies is so in-depth.

I have seen God's Law of Attraction at work in churches, too. At one church I ministered in, the pastor told me, "It is interesting that when new people come into our church, they will often come with their adult children and grandchildren and sometimes even bring their elderly parents." I discovered that many of the elders and leaders had four generations in that church. I shared with them how God's Law of Attraction was at work in attracting similar families to their congregation.

Another church I visited was full of wealthy businessmen and entrepreneurs. Sure enough, the pastor had been a successful businessman before he was called into the ministry and started the church. His first elders and board of directors were also successful businessmen. The Law of Attraction was at work as many in the business community began to attend that church.

When you are seeking relationships, it is important to understand The Law of Attraction. For example, let's say you desire to attract individuals who have a passion for helping children at risk around the world. You look around, but cannot find anyone with the same passion in your church. You think, "It would be so good if I could just find one person to connect with over this desire."

Take time to meditate on the Lord's promises such as:

"Delight yourself in the Lord; and He will give you the desires of your heart."   —Psalm 37:4

"Two are better than one because they have a good return for their labor."   —Ecclesiastes 4:9

Ask God to help you cultivate a dream in your mind about a person or persons with like passion being drawn to you. Perhaps you could even make a vision board, with pictures of individuals rallying together and happy children in the nation you have a burden for, that shows the outcome of your desires. Include statements of faith that show how children at risk will be reached through those that rally around you. Post words on your board like, "fulfilled projects," "provision," "love," "God-ideas," etc. Vision boards can be created on paper or computer. You can take photos of your vision board and carry it on your phone, too. This will keep the vision alive in your mind and heart.

The Law of Attraction will draw to you what you are thinking, imagining, and feeling. Get excited that God is drawing people of like heart and vision to you. His Law of Attraction will work on your behalf. Remember to cast down every negative or fearful thought. You do not want to attract those things. You want to attract your desire, so unleash it.

When I help single people who desire to be married, I encourage them to see themselves as an attraction magnet to the perfect partner. I exhort them to cast down every fearful thought regarding their singleness, to dream big and envision themselves attracting God's perfect mate. It works because it is God's Law of Attraction.

Your Key Relationship

The primary and most valuable relationship you have in life is with Jesus Christ. Jesus is the Savior of the world and He is the only way to the Father. In order to have relationship and harmony with God, you must receive Jesus Christ as your personal Savior and Lord. Then you can develop your relationship with Him through reading His Word, prayer, worship and devotional times. You will become acquainted with various aspects of His character and nature as you spend time with Him. When your relationship with Jesus is growing in passion, it will attract others to you who are filled with passion for Him as well.

The closest relationships I have in life are rich in the character and nature of Jesus. They are righteous, wise, moral – filled with faith, love and joy. They manifest His power and glory. These are attributes I have discovered in Jesus, as I have built relationship with Him. I attract relationships in my life that are like Jesus because I am focused in my thoughts, imaginations and emotions on Him. The Christ nature in you attracts the Christ nature in others.

"Healthy, fulfilling relationships are vital for a prosperous life. Your life is extremely rich when filled with them." —Patricia King

Summary

1. God's Law of Attraction works in the realm of relationships. You attract those with common interests, values, beliefs and goals.

2. You become like the company you keep.

3. Relationships accelerate The Law of Attraction. The more relationships you have with others who share the same interests and beliefs, the stronger and quicker the effect of The Law of Attraction is in those areas of your life.

4. Define your desire for relationship. Dream about it, think it, imagine it.

5. The primary and most valuable relationship you have in life is with Jesus Christ. When you develop a relationship with Jesus, other relationships that resemble His nature will be attracted to you. The Christ nature in you attracts the Christ nature in others.

Activation

1. If you do not know Jesus Christ in relationship and desire to give Him your heart and life, you can receive Him as Your Savior and Lord right now. Pray the following prayer:

   "Dear Lord Jesus, I believe that you are the Savior of the world who died on the cross for my sins. I repent from my sins and invite You to come into my heart, forgive my sins and give me a brand new, eternal life. I ask You to be my Savior and Lord, and to write my name in Your Book of Life in heaven. Thank You, Jesus, for coming into my heart. You are my only God and I love You. Amen."

If you prayed this prayer, Jesus came into your heart and you can now grow in relationship with Him. Talk to Him by faith. Read the Bible, especially the New Testament. As you grow in your relationship with Him you will attract other relationships that display the aspects of His nature that you focus on.

2. Make a list of the kinds of relationships you have attracted into your life. What are their character traits? Do you like these character traits? If not, what do you think has caused the attraction?

3. Make a list of the types of character traits and qualities you would like to attract in relationships. What can you do to activate The Law of Attraction to fulfill your desire?

CHAPTER EIGHT

Your Prosperous Finances

"Submit to God and be at peace with him; in this way prosperity will come to you."

Anonymous, The Pocket Companion Bible: NKJV

Your Prosperous Finances

We have seen how your soul prospers when you are filled with God's perspective. When you delight yourself in Him and act on His Word, you will attract what you are focused on in Him.

Remember that 3 John 1:2 has taught us that as our soul prospers, we can prosper in all respects. That means your finances can prosper, too. Let me illustrate this through the Scriptures and share some testimonies with you.

Two Laws Are Better Than One

I am going to share a portion of Scripture that I absolutely love! I have meditated on this Scripture, acted upon it and enjoyed the fruit of it over and over and over throughout my years of knowing Jesus. It is a Scripture that is written in the context of financial provision. Remember that you attract to yourself the things that you think on and give your attention to with your thoughts, imagination, emotions, words and actions.

"Now this I say, he who sows sparingly will also reap sparingly, and he who sows bountifully will also reap bountifully. Each one must do just as he has purposed in his heart, not grudgingly or under compulsion, for God loves a cheerful giver. And God is able to make all grace abound to you, so that always having all sufficiency in everything, you may have an abundance for every good deed... Now He who supplies seed to the sower and bread for food will supply and multiply your seed for sowing and increase the harvest of your righteousness; you will be enriched in everything for all liberality, which through us is producing thanksgiving to God."

—2 Corinthians 9:6-8, 10-11

Years ago, as a brand new Christian, I read this passage and believed it. It jumped off the page at me, and faith entered my heart concerning it. I would read it often and I still do. Remember, The Law of Attraction works for all people, all the time – just like The Law of Gravity. The Law of Attraction works for you when you activate it.

When I focus on this truth, proclaim it, and act on it, God's Law of Attraction goes to work and brings me its manifestation. Our prosperity as a family has steadily increased over the years as we have continued to sow. The Law of Sowing and Reaping is also a God-created law, so you actually have two laws working on your behalf when you embrace this promise.

Isaac and The Law of Attraction

Let's look at a biblical example God's Law of Attraction working together with The Law of Sowing and Reaping.

"Now Isaac sowed in that land and reaped in the same year a hundredfold. And the Lord blessed him, and the man became rich, and continued to grow richer until he became very wealthy." —Genesis 26:12-13

Not only did Isaac step into the Law of Sowing and Reaping, he also activated God's Law of Attraction. He was thinking about, dreaming about, and acting on what he desired in his life. God's Law of Attraction responded and drew to him what he expected. Look at the progression of how this took place:

1. Isaac sowed his seed. Farmers do not sow seed without expecting a harvest. In other words, their thoughts are processing things like, "How much and what type of seed should I plant in order to get my desired harvest?" Not only are they thinking about it, but I am sure they are imagining how great the full harvest will be and feeling the emotional excitement as they anticipate its potential. Can you see how the soul is fully engaged?

2. Isaac reaped in the same year a hundredfold. That is an amazing harvest. For every seed he sowed he received at least one hundred times that in the crop's yield. Some Bible commentaries note that the "fold" is more than one hundred times; they see it as folded over. So, if you were to sow one dollar folded over, it would be two; folded over again, it would be four; folded over again, it would be eight, etc. If you did that one hundred times, it is a huge harvest. Either way, it is fantastic! And, this all came to him in the same year.

3. And the Lord blessed him! What? A hundredfold increase is already a great blessing, but it says and the Lord blessed him. I have discovered firsthand that when I activate The Law of Attraction in one area, other areas of my life get blessed, too. In Deuteronomy 28:2 the Lord promises that blessings will come upon us and over-take us when we obey Him. The blessings come in on every wave. You become a blessing magnet.

4. And Isaac became rich. Isaac became rich when he sowed seed with expectation and delight. Not only did it yield a hundred-fold that year, but other areas of his life were also blessed. Isaac lived in a perpetual and increasing state of abundance, all because God blessed the seed Isaac sowed in faith through His Laws of Sowing and Reaping and Attraction.

Being rich is different from being blessed. I could cut you a check for $1,000 right now and you would be blessed, but you would not be rich. Being rich is when you live in a sustained state of "more than enough." Many believers compare *rich* to the standards of the world, but the realm of being rich in the kingdom is different than the world because it is not measured by dollars and cents. For example, I am rich because I have more than enough to meet my needs. I live in that realm. It is not up and down – it is sustained. My focus and trust are not on money. There is no money in heaven because money is a world-system currency. God plus nothing equals everything I need. When God and His promises become your focus and the love of your life, then you will always attract more than enough – and there is no sweat to it, either.

5. And Isaac continued to grow richer. The Law of Attraction begins with a seed sown with intention, then it continues to attract more and more so you increase exponentially – when you expect it.

6. Until he became very wealthy. Being wealthy is different from being rich. Being rich is about you living in a state of abundance, but wealth is when you influence the world around you with your provision and gifts. Again, kingdom wealth is not just measured in dollars and cents.

I have seen God's Law of Attraction work in the same way it did for Isaac – and it can work for you, too. When you combine The Law of Sowing and Reaping and The Law of Attraction, you are set up for a huge blessing.

I have more in-depth teaching on this subject in my books, *Step into Supernatural Provision*, *Create Your World* and *In the Zone*, listed in the back of this book.

One time, I was believing for the fulfillment of a ministry project that we still needed $100,000 to complete. I sowed a $1,000 seed, believing for the $100,000 to manifest in that year. I sowed the seed on October 29th and the $100,000 manifested less than three weeks later. Plus, more blessings were loosed at the same time and following. An investment my husband and I were waiting for also got released within those three weeks, and every week more unexpected blessings poured into our lives.

Intentionality is a key. You will notice in 2 Corinthians 9:7 that God loves a cheerful giver. This is emotional joy and expectation. It unlocks The Law of Attraction for you. That's why God loves cheerful giving so much. He loves what it does for you. It attracts blessing. If you have fear when you are sowing, or you are giving grudgingly, you will not attract blessing – you will attract lack. You attract what is in your heart.

Jesus and The Law of Attraction

Another great example of The Law of Attraction at work is in the story of Jesus miraculously multiplying the fish and the loaves in Mark 6:33-44.

Five thousand spiritually hungry people had been sitting on a hillside all day, listening to Jesus teach. It was getting late, so the disciples suggested that they send the crowd away to get something to eat. Jesus had a different idea. He said, "You give them something to eat." You will note that the disciples did not come into immediate agreement with Jesus. They struggled with doubt and unbelief because they were looking at what they didn't have, rather than what they did have. Jesus, however, turned their attention around and said, "How many loaves do you have? Go, look." This is a different perspective. The disciples were thinking lack, but Jesus was thinking abundance.

Sometimes we need to "go look" at what we do have, so we can position ourselves for a miracle. Even if we think we have nothing, the Scripture teaches that God will supply seed for us to sow (2 Corinthians 9:10).

The disciples returned and presented Jesus with five loaves and two fish. They might have wondered how this little offering was going to feed the crowd that was before them, but look what Jesus did. He turned His focus to heaven. He knew He needed a miracle, so He turned His focus heavenward and He blessed the food. Too often, we curse our provision by saying, "Oh we don't have enough, times are tough, etc." Jesus' thoughts and focus were on the miracle so He blessed what was in His hand. He then broke the bread apart and began to distribute it. He was acting on what He believed. He was expecting a miracle.

The Scripture says that He kept on giving. In other words, this miracle was a replenishment miracle. Jesus was teaching His disciples to work this type of miracle. Every time they gave someone in the crowd something to eat, it replenished in their hand. The Law of Attraction was attracting a miracle because that was what Jesus expected. That is what filled His mind and focus.

The loaves and fish continued to replenish until at some point they began to multiply. After they had fed over five thousand people, there were twelve full baskets left over. Notice that the miracle took place as they continued to give away the little they had in their hand. The catering truck did not show up with food for everyone, but God did!

The miracle is in your hand. You can attract the miracle realm of provision when you keep giving away what is in your hand. The Lord will replenish it and, at some point, it will begin to increase and multiply. What an awesome way to live!

Elijah and The Law of Attraction

God sent Elijah to a widow during a great famine, revealing prophetically that the widow would provide for him (1 Kings 17:8-9). Elijah's thoughts and corresponding actions were in agreement with God's word, so God's Law of Attraction was activated. When Elijah arrived, he asked the widow to bring him a jar of water to drink and a piece of bread to eat.

> "But she said, 'As the Lord your God lives, I have no bread, only a handful of flour in the bowl and a little oil in the jar; and behold, I am gathering a few sticks that I may go in and prepare for me and my son, that we may eat it and die.'"
>
> —1 Kings 17:12

The widow was in a dangerous place. Her thoughts and belief that she and her son were about to eat their last meal and then die could have attracted what she believed, but God intervened. He sent Elijah to decree the will of God for her and her son.

> "Then Elijah said to her, 'Do not fear; go, do as you have said, but make me a little bread cake from it first and bring it out to me, and afterward you may make one for yourself and for your son. For thus says the Lord God of Israel, 'The bowl of flour shall not be exhausted, nor shall the jar of oil be empty, until the day that the Lord sends rain on the face of the earth.'"
> —1 Kings 17:13-14

The Lord was shifting the condition of her soul from discouragement and negativity to faith. She believed the word of the Lord, acted upon it and saw miracles of replenishment as "she and he and her household ate for many days" (1 Kings 17:15). Her shift in belief and action activated The Law of Attraction.

Our Breaker Team Partners often report financial increase and miracles when they sow unto the Lord in our ministry, because our ministry believes that they will be blessed. Our prayers, decrees, thoughts and expectations for our partners' prosperity attracts increase for them. You can stand in the gap for your loved ones in this way, too. You were created to be blessed and to be a blessing.

Just like Elijah was used to intervene in the case of the widow, you too can help others have their breakthrough. Elijah was used to turn around the widow's beliefs and then The Law of Attraction went to work. All of us in Christ can do the same.

Your financial prosperity flows from the thoughts, emotions and beliefs in your soul that are aligned with God's promises of provision. May you prosper as your soul prospers.

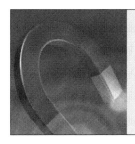

"Financial prosperity requires faith and action. Believe the truth God speaks into your heart and act on it." —Patricia King

Summary

1. God desires for you to financially prosper, as your soul prospers.

2. When you align your soul with God's instruction and promises for financial prosperity, you activate God's Law of Attraction.

3. When you believe and activate God's Word regarding sowing and reaping, The Law of Attraction and The Law of Sowing and Reaping will work together on your behalf.

4. When you believe and activate God's promises and instruction for financial increase and multiplication, the Law of Attraction will attract the miracle realm to you.

5. When you give away what is in your hand and believe for more, replenishment miracles will be attracted to you.

6. Your financial prosperity flows from the thoughts, emotions and beliefs in your soul that are aligned with God's promises of provision.

Activation

1. With intentionality, sow a financial seed into a ministry that is "good ground" – a ministry that has pure faith for increase, good stewardship of God's funds and effective outreach.

2. Mark the day you sowed that seed and wait with expectation for replenishment and then multiplication.

3. Water the seed with decrees from the Word of God, praise and thanksgiving.

4. Journal the results.

5. Testify to others.

CHAPTER NINE

Words and Action

"By getting the Word deep into your spirit and speaking it out boldly, you release spiritual power to change things in natural circumstances."   —Kenneth Copeland

Words and Action

The Power of Words

> "For out of the abundance of the heart the mouth speaks."
>
> —Matthew 12:34 (NKJV)

The mouth speaks what is in the heart. Remember that "heart" is another word for "soul." When your soul is in agreement and alignment with God's truth, then your mouth will speak life-giving words that create your world.

Your words carry power and will either curse or bless your life. No word is without effect, and every word we speak fills the earth with what is spoken. Knowing this should create great reverence for God and cause us to be very watchful of what comes through our lips.

> "Death and life are in the power of the tongue, and they who indulge in it shall eat the fruit of it [for death or life]."
>
> —Proverbs 18:21 (AMP)

Your words produce death or life and your mouth speaks out what is in your soul. You attract what you are thinking, imagining, feeling and speaking. The material world is attracted to what you are focused on.

Let's review how The Law of Attraction works:

1. You think on something, perhaps a desire or an idea.

2. Your thoughts produce images in your imagination.

3. Your thoughts and images produce feelings in your emotions.

4. Your will chooses to accept the thoughts/imaginations/feelings.

5. Your mouth then speaks what you have chosen through your will.

6. What you thought, imagined, felt and spoke is attracted to you.

Words are spiritual. They carry power. Jesus said, "But I say to you that for every idle word men may speak, they will give account of it in the day of judgment. For by your words you will be justified, and by your words you will be condemned." Matthew 12:36-37 (NKJV)

God created the world through words (Genesis 1:3), and He created us with the ability to choose our own words and speak them forth at will.

"By faith we understand that the worlds were framed by the word of God, so that the things which are seen were not made of things which are visible."   Hebrews 11:3 (NKJV)

In other words, when God declared a creative word into the spirit, it created the manifestation of what was spoken. You are made in God's image and likeness. Your words also carry power to create, but your words can also destroy. James 3:2-12 teaches that the words we speak direct the course of our life and can produce blessing or curse.

The words you speak attract blessing or curse. Be careful what comes out of your mouth. Let your mouth speak words of life that flow from a soul that is aligned to the promises of God and watch The Law of Attraction go to work for you.

Establishing Results

We can be thankful that just because we think, feel, or speak something once, it will not necessarily manifest. If that were so, every time we had a negative thought or emotion, or let a negative word slip out of our mouth, it would materialize.

Nevertheless, we know for sure that every word we speak has some effect. The more thoughts, images, feelings and words you release, the more they materialize. The more intentional you are, the quicker they manifest.

With this understanding, it is important to regularly repent from thoughts, feelings and words that are contrary to God's truth, and only think, feel, and speak things that are aligned to His will and purposes.

Established thoughts, feelings and words bring forth established manifestation. You can build established results through intentionally choosing your thoughts, images, feelings and words.

The Power of God's Word

God's Word is final authority, and when you proclaim His Word it goes into the realm of the spirit and begins to create and attract to your life what it is sent to do. Read the following amazing Scriptures that reveal the power of the Word of God.

"For with God nothing is ever impossible and no word from God shall be without power or impossible of fulfillment."
—Luke 1:37 (AMP)

"For as the rain comes down, and the snow from heaven, and do not return there, but water the earth, and make it bring forth and bud, that it may give seed to the sower and bread to the eater, so shall My word be that goes forth from My mouth; It shall not return to Me void, but it shall accomplish what I please, and it shall prosper in the thing for which I sent it."
Isaiah 55:10-11 (NKJV)

"For the Word that God speaks is alive and full of power [making it active, operative, energizing, and effective]..."
Hebrews 4:12 (AMP)

These Scriptures powerfully confirm God's Law of Attraction. When you proclaim God's Word, it goes to work on your behalf and returns to you what it was sent to do. It attracts to you what it represents.

I really believe in the power of scriptural decrees. Decree the Word of God every day and watch as you attract to your life what you are proclaiming. Proclaiming the Word fills your soul with rich truth. It prospers your soul and therefore attracts results.

The Power of Action

When you act upon what your soul believes, it attracts according to the action. For example, I believe that when I sow, I reap. This belief is firmly established in my heart. I think it, I imagine it, I feel it, I speak it – but I also act on it.

If I only thought, imagined, felt and spoke it, but did not activate, there would be no landing strip for The Law of Attraction to land on. I would have equity in the unseen realm through my thoughts, but I would be lacking action.

Let's say, for example, I desired a specific employment position. I could pray about it, dream about it, believe that I will get chosen for it, and decree with words that it is mine, but if I do not act on the desire by submitting my resume, there is no connection for God's Law of Attraction to release the fulfillment.

Your actions are important. They activate God's Law of Attraction. I could share testimony after testimony after testimony of how abundance has been attracted to my life because I have believed and acted upon God's promises of abundant harvest for abundant sowing.

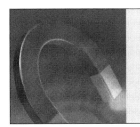

"Faith without works is dead, so activate your faith with your works and produce life in you, for you, and through you." —Patricia King

Summary

1. The mouth speaks what is in the heart (soul). When your soul is in agreement and alignment with God's truth, then the mouth will speak life-giving words that create your world.

2. Your words carry power and will attract either curse or blessing to your life. No word is without effect. Every word we speak fills the earth with what is spoken.

3. This is how The Law of Attraction works:

   1. You think on something, perhaps a desire or an idea.

   2. Your thoughts produce images in your imagination.

   3. Your thoughts and images produce feelings in your emotions.

   4. Your will chooses to accept the thoughts/imaginations/feelings.

   5. Your mouth then speaks what you have chosen through your will.

   6. What you thought, imagined, felt, and spoke is attracted to you.

4. Just because you think, feel, or speak something once, it will not necessarily manifest. However, know for sure that every word you speak has some effect. The more thoughts, images, feelings and words you release, the more they materialize. The more intentional you are, the quicker they manifest.

5. Proclamation of God's Word is one of the most powerful ways to attract the will of God into your life and prosper your soul.

6. Your actions are important. They activate God's Law of Attraction.

7. When you act upon what your soul believes, it attracts according to the action.

Activation

1. Make intentional daily decrees of the Word of God into one specific area of your life that you want to be blessed.

2. What actions can you take in order to attract results? Write them out.

3. Perform the actions and anticipate results.

CHAPTER TEN

Realms and Atmospheres

"Your environment can mold and transform you, or you can mold and transform your environment." —Anonymous

Realms and Atmospheres

The Story of Daniel

Daniel lived in the midst of an extremely oppressive environment. God's people had disobeyed and rebelled against the Lord for many years. In spite of many warnings and clear prophetic calls to righteousness, they had continued in their evil ways.

As a result, God placed them under the control of Babylon, the most brutal heathen nation of that day. By their choices and actions, they had attracted this environment and realm of bondage. They lived in a horrible atmosphere of severe oppression, poverty, and hopelessness because they had departed from the Lord in their hearts and minds.

Daniel was a young man who had not made the sinful choices that had brought judgment upon his nation. Yet, he too lived in the oppressive spiritual atmosphere of Babylon. Even though the consequences of his people's sins were all around him, they did not affect him. Daniel lived in a different realm and atmosphere. Instead of defeat, he lived in the glory of God's goodness, wisdom and favor.

Daniel created realms and atmospheres in his life that were full of opportunities and testimonies. While others toiled under terrible sin and oppression, Daniel lived in an environment of God's righteousness. He was a godly influence on the key leaders of his day, wrote glorious testimonies, had encounters with God and created prophetic journals that eventually became part of the Bible.

Even when he was unjustly thrown into a den of lions, Daniel created a realm of peace through his faith and trust in God that caused even the lions to yield to his angel-enforced atmosphere. Wise thoughts, beliefs, words, choices and actions flowed from Daniel's love relationship with God to create realms and atmospheres of victory, purpose and promise despite the difficult times and repressive environment in which he lived. The Law of Attraction responded to Daniel's focus and faith and attracted an atmosphere of favor, purpose, promise, and grace.

Like Daniel, you also can attract and create such environments in the midst of your own lions of despair, darkness, and defeat. You might live in an oppressed environment but it doesn't have to affect you. You can live in a different realm. You can attract freedom, success, abundance, and victory. It all depends on the posture of your soul. If your soul prospers by being aligned with God's truth and purposes, then the environment and realm you live in will be one of prosperity in every respect – regardless of what is going on around you.

Realms Defined

A realm is a territory (visible or invisible) over which rule or control is exercised. For example: An operations manager in a company can administer his or her realm of responsibility with a spirit of excellence; or, the worship of a congregation can activate angels in the unseen realm and cause many to experience supernatural encounters.

A realm can also be defined as something that dominates. For example: The realm of God's tangible glory prevailed in the meeting; or, a realm of success dominated the life of Mr. Jones.

Atmospheres Defined

An atmosphere is a general pervasive feeling or mood. For example: An atmosphere of elation. It can also describe a special mood, tone or character that is associated with a specific place or geographic location. For example, a city can feel gloomy or someone's home can feel peaceful.

Atmospheres can include the tone of your life or a situation. You can feel atmospheres. For example, you might walk into a church meeting and sense an atmosphere of faith and anticipation. The faith and anticipation of the leaders and those in attendance attracted this atmosphere. The same is true of the opposite. I have walked into meetings where there was a clear atmosphere of skepticism and unbelief. You could feel it in the air. The doubts and fears of those in attendance attracted that atmosphere.

The Law of Attraction Responds to Realms and Atmospheres

When I first moved to the Phoenix area of Arizona, I noticed a strong resistance in the spiritual atmosphere to the prophetic and the supernatural. This was confirmed by many leaders who told me that the region was known as a "graveyard for prophets." They shared detailed stories of many prophets and ministers in the supernatural who were either driven out of the region or had died there.

There is a difference between fact and truth. Fact is based on the temporal realm, but truth is based on the eternal realm. Truth will always trump fact when you choose to align your thoughts, beliefs, and feelings to it. In this case, the truth was that God had called us to Phoenix to establish Extreme Prophetic (XP Ministries) as a global distribution portal for the realm of the prophetic and the supernatural. The fact was, the spiritual atmosphere was thick with resistance.

Once an atmosphere or a realm is established, The Law of Attraction will continue to attract more of the same. That stronghold will get stronger without intervention.

I chose to believe that God wanted to create a new atmosphere in the Phoenix area and eventually establish a whole new realm for that region. So, I hosted prophetic gatherings, schools of the prophetic, prophetic evangelism outreaches, built a studio in the region to produce my television program Extreme Prophetic (renamed Everlasting Love following the breakthrough), wrote books and curriculums on the prophetic and the supernatural, and founded XP Media as a media network for the prophetic and the supernatural.

I locked in until my beliefs, prayers, words and actions attracted people hungry for the prophetic and the supernatural. Today, Phoenix is attracting many prophets and ministries who love the supernatural. It has become a spiritual watering hole, and millions worldwide are being reached with the prophetic and supernatural through our ministry there, alongside many other wonderful, strong, and healthy ministries and churches who express fullness of kingdom life and doctrine. The atmosphere changed. A new realm was established.

Be Careful What You Identify With

If you allow it, the negative effects of realms and atmospheres can affect you also. In the business world, for example, certain atmospheres can limit people in their calling. An executive who works his or her way up in a company may discover that there is a corporate ceiling. If that person remains in that company, he or she might have to live under the restriction of that ceiling. The realm of that company is confining him or her to that level. They may need to find a company that is functioning in a greater realm in order to break into a new level.

Almost thirty years ago, I met a young man in his thirties who was full of charisma, faith, and confidence, with a clear calling to the inner city. Our team was helping him reach the lost and the bound in his region. There was joy and excitement as we served on the streets together, observing the power and love of God at work. This young minister was always so fresh, optimistic and faith-filled. He had grown up in an upper-middle class family and wore the confidence of that upbringing.

About twenty years later, I met up with him again. He was still ministering in the inner city and was fruitful in winning people to Christ. He still had a pastoral and evangelistic anointing on him for the people on the streets. But something had changed – he had taken on the environment. He looked and talked like someone from the inner city. He carried the oppressive mindsets and atmosphere that mark that environment. He did not look much different from those he was reaching out to. I could no longer tell the difference between him and those he was ministering to. By being in that atmosphere day after day, he had eventually attracted the realm to himself.

What you look upon, you can become. Remember the story of Jacob and the flocks (see Genesis 30:31-43). The flocks looked on rods that were striped and spotted and so they reproduced according to what they focused on.

Be careful what you place yourself under or identify with. Never forget that you are a child of the Living God, His royal ambassador, a king and a priest for Him in the earth. When you go into oppressed atmospheres, do not identify with those atmospheres – identify with your heavenly home. In any atmosphere, only identify with the truth of God's Word, because what you allow in your mind, heart, and desires is attracted to you.

Drink-In Godly Atmospheres

When I go into a church filled with God's glory and presence, I purposely choose to drink-in that atmosphere and invite the realm of His presence to fill me. You can intentionally receive from any atmosphere.

Once, I was ministering in a city with great prosperity. I deliberately chose to receive the regional prosperity that was rooted in God. I am selective about what I allow into my heart. When I see opulence, for example, I am not going to identify with any sin that might be at work behind it, but I will identify with God's perfection in heavenly places and begin to draw from the opulence of His holy realm.

The natural atmospheres around you can lead you to meditate on the Scriptures, through which you can identify with all the blessings that God gave Abraham, David and Solomon in the area of prosperity and glory. When I take time in the Lord to identify with His opulence, I begin to attract that realm to my life. The more you meditate on it, the more you will attract it. This is The Law of Attraction.

There are geographical places in the earth that carry realms of certain anointings and kingdom expressions. For example, Redding, California, is known through Bill Johnson's ministry as a city that manifests a realm of kingdom culture. People who move there or spend extended periods of time there get filled with that realm. They become connected to it in the atmosphere of the place. The Law of Attraction is at work.

Our ministry intentionally and officially belongs to three apostolic networks. The reason is because each of the networks excel uniquely in a certain aspect of kingdom advancement. When I attend meetings in these networks, I drink-in the spiritual environment. I sow into the networks with my finances, prayers and service, and as a result attract the realm of authority that has been carved out by them.

You Can Create Realms and Atmospheres

You can create atmospheres and realms in your life by activating The Law of Attraction. For example, let's say there is an atmosphere of strife in your home. Those who live in the home created it. If you do not intentionally change it, The Law of Attraction will continue to respond to strife and attract more until your home is locked into a realm of strife. With intentionality you can begin to create a different realm – a realm of love and peace in your home through what you choose to focus on, imagine, speak and activate.

You do not have to simply let life take its course. You can design it according to God's blueprint for success and prosperity. Remember that you are attracting something to your life all the time. It is the way God's Law of Attraction works. Intentionally position your soul to align itself with God's truth and ways so you can attract the goodness of the Lord in every realm of your life.

"Anyone who is offered the choice to live a life flourishing in the abundance of God's goodness or to live in oppression, lack, and despair, would definitely choose to live the flourishing life. I know of no one who would choose the latter. Why then do so many live the latter?"
—*Patricia King*

Summary

1. Atmospheres and realms can influence you.

2. You can intentionally receive from realms and atmospheres.

3. When you understand The Law of Attraction you can intentionally work it to benefit your life.

4. The Law of Attraction responds to realms and atmospheres.

5. You can create realms and atmospheres.

Activation

1. Observe an area of your life where you are struggling or producing bad fruit/results. Examine, with the Holy Spirit, the possibilities of how the struggle or the bad fruit was attracted to you. Make a list of what the Spirit reveals to you.

2. With intentionality, make a plan to change it so you will attract breakthrough and good fruit.

3. Make a list of atmospheres and realms that you would like to create in your life.

CHAPTER ELEVEN

Dealing with Crisis

"The ultimate measure of a man is not where he stands in moments of comfort and convenience, but where he stands at times of challenge and controversy."

—Rev. Dr. Martin Luther King, Jr.

God Wants Us to Attract Breakthroughs

A number of years ago, I was in the midst of a major crisis. Crisis always demands attention and focus and usually gives ample opportunity for fear and doubt to fill our thoughts and emotions. I was anxious, sad, and losing sleep. The more I tried to fix the problems, the more the problems grew in size and number.

Finally, a good friend and one of my treasured advisors said to me, "Patricia, just lay it down and carry on with life. The problem with trying to fix this right now is that it is taking on a life of its own and if you are not careful, it will consume you." The Spirit of God impacted me powerfully through that infusion of wisdom. From that point on in that situation, I looked at God's solutions and not at the problems. I fixed my mind on His ability to sort it all out. I stepped out of the swirls in my mind and instead praised Him and thanked Him for the forthcoming victory.

I did not understand God's Law of Attraction at that time, but the effects of it were evident. When my thoughts went to the crisis, I attracted more crisis. When my thoughts went to the solution and hope, I attracted breakthrough. God's Law of Attraction was working. The cycle of crisis ended and I was kept strong in the midst of it. No wonder the Scripture teaches us to "count it all joy" when we face various trials and testings (James 1:2 NKJV). God wants us to attract breakthroughs, not more trials.

Don't Identify Yourself with Crisis

A couple was offered help to get through a difficult time in their life, but when they shared their story with the counselor, it became evident that their "difficult time" had lasted for more than 15 years. The couple had been severely oppressed with one mishap after another, year after year. The counselor released a word of wisdom for them. "Do not focus on your problems. Do not talk about them. Ignore them and only look at the good life you have. Only praise the Lord for all the great things. Praise Him for the solution He is going to bring. Deny entrance of negative, fearful and anxious thoughts or feelings. Believe for a good outcome."

This couple's troubles were severe and very real – definitely not a figment of their imagination. But the bigger problem the counselor had uncovered was that they had identified themselves with crisis. Every crisis they faced filled them with fear and anxiety. They would say things like, "This has gone on for so long, will it ever end? Everything goes bad for us no matter what we do. We are doing all the right things but we only have bad results. We just get over one hurdle and we get hit with something else."

Do you see what I see? The Law of Attraction was activated and it responded to their negative expectations and fear-based thoughts, emotions, and words. They would never get out of their situation unless they committed to attracting the right response. God's Law of Attraction was available for them to utilize for the good, but they could not see it. They did not believe it and as a result did not get their breakthrough. Sadly, to this day that couple is still swirling in crisis. They are addicted to it and are identified by it.

In times of crisis you must remember who you are. Do not let the crisis define you as an oppressed individual. No! You are a child of the King. You are an overcomer. You are more than a conqueror. Look at the glorious expected end and attract your victory. With God on your side, you cannot lose! Remember who you are and remember how great God is in the midst of the battle.

Receive Encouragement from the Lord

Your victory over crisis begins with the prosperity of your soul. Your soul is prosperous when it is aligned with God's Word, ways, and truth. If you are facing a crisis right now, don't get absorbed in the crisis. If you fill your soul with all the horrible aspects of the crisis, you will attract more crisis. Instead, go into the presence of the Lord and receive encouragement from Him. Remember He is the God of all encouragement. He already knows that you will come through with flying colors if you trust Him. When He gives you promises, write them out in a journal and keep yourself encouraged in them when you are tempted by discouragement. Stay encouraged.

Make sure that you surround yourself with faith-filled, optimistic friends, too. In a crisis, you don't need to be around pessimistic people who are in agreement with how terrible things are. Stay away from them. Jesus put the mourners out of the room before He raised Jairus' daughter from the dead (Luke 8:51-52). He knew that He only needed faith-filled people around Him in the midst of that situation.

Fill Your Thoughts, Imagination, and Emotions with Visions of Victory

Winston Churchill was facing a national crisis in the Second World War when England was under threat. He did not give in to negative possibilities of defeat or bad reports that were coming in from every side, but instead he stood up and delivered a decree to the nation that aligned their focus with victory:

"We shall go on to the end... we shall fight with growing confidence and growing strength... we shall defend our island, whatever the cost may be. We shall fight on the beaches, we shall fight on the landing grounds, we shall fight in the fields and in the streets, we shall fight in the hills; we shall never surrender..."

Winston Churchill activated God's Law of Attraction, and the war was won.

Whatever you focus on, you empower. And, you get to choose what you focus on. Take time to sit back and meditate on the victory that will follow the crisis. Fill your thoughts with promises of God's goodness and your imagination with visions of how it will look when you are in total victory. Fill your soul with alignment to God's goodness. Let your soul prosper.

If negative and fearful thoughts attempt to invade your mind, cast them down as quickly as you identify them and replace them with thoughts of victory and breakthrough. Imagine yourself sharing the great testimony of God's power that brought you through victorious. As you think godly thoughts and imagine godly vision, your emotions will also begin to align. Your soul is becoming prosperous, and when your soul is prosperous by aligning to God's will, you will flourish and succeed. This is God's Law of Attraction. It works for all people all the time. It will work for you.

Decree God's Word into Your Crisis

In faith, decree God's promises into your crisis. Remember that God's Word does not return void but it accomplishes everything it is sent to do (Isaiah 55:11). You can destroy the crisis by decreeing the word of victory into it. The Word of God when it is decreed will build a framework of victory in the spirit realm that will attract blessing to it.

Praise Changes the Atmosphere

Praise is so powerful in the midst of crisis. In Acts 16, we read about Paul and Silas in prison. I would say that they were in a bit of a crisis, but they had a different perspective. Instead, they saw it as an opportunity. Your perspective is everything in the midst of crisis.

Paul and Silas were praising the Lord in the midst of being beaten and thrown in prison. They had their focus on God and His glorious victory. As a result, a great miracle of God came through an earthquake and set not only them but all the prisoners in that jail free. Now that is a turnaround!

Praise is one of your most powerful weapons in crisis. Praise attracts the Lord's power in your situation and will change the atmosphere.

Live Like a Winner

If you believe that you are a winner, then live like one. Put a little skip in your step. Choose to leap out of bed in the morning with expectation for the crisis to be settled. It will be, you just have to stay in joy and peace during the process. Keep reminding yourself of the great and victorious completion of the cycle. Make choices to overcome in every situation you face. Your actions released in faith will bring about great results. God will give you wisdom if you ask for it. He will give you all the action steps you need to win. When He speaks wisdom to you, activate it! Feel like a winner. Talk like a winner. Walk like a winner. Live like a winner. Why? Because you are a winner.

Your actions will attract your breakthrough. You were not created to live in a realm of oppressive crisis. You were created to experience one victory after another. It is who you are and what you were made for. Press in with joy. Make the crisis work for you, not against you. You can do it!

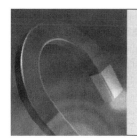

"If you don't quit you win. You are a winner, so live to win."   *—Patricia King*

Summary

1. The enemy comes to bring crisis, but God comes to bring victory.

2. The Law of Attraction can attract increased crisis or victory, depending on what you fill your soul with.

3. Focusing on crisis empowers and multiplies crisis.

4. When you are in crisis, receive encouragement from the Lord, and gather people of encouragement around you.

5. Deny negative thoughts and imaginations in crisis and fill your thoughts, imaginations and emotions with visions of victory.

6. Decree the Word of God into crisis.

7. Praise changes the atmosphere.

8. Live like a winner. Your actions attract breakthrough.

Activation

Identify a crisis or challenge in your life. Activate the keys in this chapter for attracting your victory:

1. Receive encouragement from the Lord. Write out the promises He gives you.

2. Surround yourself with people of faith and encouragement.

3. Deny negative thoughts and imaginations and fill your thoughts, imaginations and emotions with visions of victory.

4. Decree the Word of God into your crisis or challenge.

5. Praise God for the breakthrough.

6. Ask God for wisdom on how to choose actions that will secure your victory.

7. Live like a winner.

CHAPTER TWELVE

Dream Big

"One of the most valuable benefits of vision is that it acts like a magnet – attracting, challenging and uniting..."

—John C. Maxwell

Dream Big

G od has put the capacity in you to dream. The desires that well up within you are important to Him and when you delight in the Lord, He will give you the desires (dreams, visions) of your heart (Psalm 37:4).

Your soul is where dreams are conceived. They grow and develop in your soul in the same way that a baby grows in the womb of its mother. The Bible teaches, "Where there is no vision, the people perish" Proverbs 29:18 (KJV). It is important for your soul's prosperity to dream and then to pursue your dreams. If you will dare to dream, you will attract the manifestation of your dreams. God's Law of Attraction will work on your behalf to fulfill them.

Receiving Your Dreams

Take time to dream. Intentionally carve out some time to ponder and define the desires of your heart. It helps to have a pen and paper available to write out your dreams. Invite the Lord to inspire you and to lead you as you dream. To help you define your dreams, ask yourself questions, such as:

1. What would I love to do if I had all the resources and people that I needed and absolutely no limitations? Write down what comes to your mind.

2. What are the specific details I would like to see fulfilled in each of my dreams? Make a list of the specifics.

3. What would my life look like if my dreams were fulfilled? Let this play out in your imagination. Dream big. Journal what you see.

4. What benefits would come into my life and the lives of others if my dreams were fulfilled? Write them out and meditate on them.

5. As you continue dreaming, take note of your emotions. What emotions are you feeling? Are you feeling joy, expectation, faith? Or, are you feeling overwhelmed, doubtful, fearful, etc.?

If your emotions are negative, then ask yourself why. God's Law of Attraction responds to your emotions, so you want them to be positive. God is full of joy, expectation, and faith. When your emotions are in line with His, your soul prospers and His Law of Attraction will respond to bring you the results. If your emotions are negative, perhaps there is a wound in your soul, like a bad emotional memory, that needs to be healed; or perhaps your faith does not connect to the dream in your heart because it is too big to grasp. In that case, try "downsizing" your dream until your faith connects with it and it is believable to you.

Cultivating Your Dreams

Now that you have identified your dreams and they are written down, meditate on them and continue to seek the Lord for His endorsement and promises concerning them. You are God's child, He wants to walk with you to fulfill your dreams. The more you think on your dreams and imagine the outcome, the more you activate The Law of Attraction.

You may find it encouraging to create a "dream board" so that you can have a visual in front of you. In February of 1980, my husband and I visited the Youth With A Mission (YWAM) base in Kona, Hawaii. Being there sparked a desire in us to attend their Discipleship Training School (DTS). We prayed and felt the Lord's pleasure on the idea. We also received confirmation through the Scriptures and our spiritual advisors. That gave us confidence to believe that we would be accepted into the school that fall.

We had only six months to get everything in order. Our two boys were young at the time (ages 5 and 6), so it would be quite a logistical feat to pull it all together. We also needed finances for the tuition, airfares, and accommodation, plus everything that still had to be looked after back home during the time we would be away. At the time, we did not have the available resources in sight. It all looked pretty overwhelming, but the dream would not leave us and we knew that faith was our currency.

I made a dream board from poster paper with the photos I had taken of Ron and I at the Hawaiian base, including the venue that hosted the children's program for our sons, with a headline: YWAM DTS KONA SEPTEMBER 1980. At the bottom of the board I posted, "Delight yourself in the Lord; and He will give you the desires of your heart." I taped the dream board to the fridge so that all day long, each and every day, I was reminded of our dream.

Ron and I also filled out the application for the school, as if we were going and began to share the vision with others. Every day we would talk about our dream, think our dream, imagine our dream. God's Law of Attraction went to work for us and that September our family was in Hawaii for the DTS. What looked impossible in the natural was made manifest. All things are possible in Christ.

This is yet another example of how The Law of Attraction works. It started with a desire that filled our thoughts, imaginations and emotions. After receiving a "green light" from the Lord, we chose to dream and to focus on the possibility of this desire coming to pass. We spent time pondering it and gazing on the "dream board" we made. We spoke about it because the words we speak activate The Law of Attraction. And, finally, we put action to our dream. These actions attracted the fulfillment. God's Law of Attraction responded.

Moving Big Dreams Forward One Step at a Time

Sometimes a dream is so big that it is wise to break it down into smaller steps that you can focus on, one at a time. For example, I have a dream to annihilate modern day slavery in our lifetime – specifically the sex trafficking of children. That is a big dream, so I have begun to fulfill a smaller dream as a step towards it.

I began by hosting an outreach school in Pattaya, Thailand. I prayed into it, meditated on it, imagined it, and got excited about it. I then moved forward to host it. The first school was a great success, and that first step attracted the next one. Before long, we were entrenched on the ground in Asia, reaching out to children at risk and attracting people from all over the world with like vision.

Within a few years, this ministry has exploded. We now have many projects in the field and are networked with others who are working toward the same dream. The Law of Attraction is what built the momentum. I can't fulfill the bigger vision by myself, but I can step into a smaller one that contributes towards the fulfillment of the bigger one.

Do not despise the days of small beginnings. As you seek the Lord, He will give you wisdom and faith to move forward. Your spirit will witness with you where your faith connects. Sometimes it is better to have a smaller vision that you know you can fulfill and then take steps forward from the momentum that is built by your initial success.

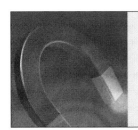

"If you can dream it, you can do it."
—Walt Disney

The Power of Self-Discipline

Dreams sometimes require self-discipline and sacrifice to fulfill. Olympic athletes, for example, have a dream to win a gold metal. Most athletes are trained in The Law of Attraction by professional coaches and sports psychologists who know the importance of aligning their thoughts, imaginations, emotions, words, and actions with their dreams of being a champion. The mental and emotional aspects of their training are as important as the physical regime required for these athletes to reach their goal.

Self-discipline is a key element for athletes. They don't always feel like training, but they know the importance of commitment. Self-discipline is an activation of the will, which is part of the soul. When your will chooses self-discipline to achieve your God-endorsed dreams, your soul prospers.

It has been discovered that when an individual disciplines themselves to fulfill a daily physical exercise regime, the ability to be disciplined in other areas of their life comes more easily. A commitment to focus on self-discipline in one area sets The Law of Attraction in motion to attract self-discipline in other areas of your life.

A business executive who desires to achieve a sales goal is another example of someone who will need to pursue self-discipline with their time and efforts in order to activate The Law of Attraction. Self-discipline is required to achieve your dreams.

Dream and Live

"Now to Him who is able to do exceedingly abundantly above all that we ask or think, according to the power that works in us..." Ephesians 3:20 (NKJV)

When people stop dreaming, they stop living. So dream big and allow The Law of Attraction to respond to those dreams, desires, and goals. God wants you to dream with Him, and He wants to fulfill your dreams – so go for it!

"Beloved, I pray that in all respects you may prosper and be in good health, just as your soul prospers."   —3 John 1:2

Go now with confident expectation into your tomorrows. Prosper in all respects and be in health. Attract His goodness and glory to your life all of your days. It truly is His will and desire for you. Choose life.

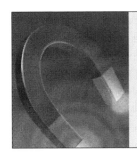

"Faith is heaven's currency. If you have faith, you can possess your God-confirmed dream."   —Patricia King

Summary

1. God has given you the capacity to dream.

2. Your soul is where your dreams are conceived and cultivated.

3. Posture yourself to receive dreams, desires and vision from the Lord.

4. Identify and define your dreams.

5. Cultivate your dreams by meditating on them, pondering them, imagining them and speaking about them.

6. Dreams require self-discipline and sacrifice to be fulfilled.

Activation

Identify a dream that you would like fulfilled in your life.

1. Write your dream in a journal where you can refer to it.

2. Ask God to confirm it.

3. Meditate on your dream. Think on it. Imagine it. Feel the reality of it.

4. Make a "dream board" that reminds you of your dream.

5. If your dream is too big to handle all at once, work on a smaller dream that contributes to the bigger one. Clearly define the smaller one.

6. Act on your dream by making a plan of action to fulfill it.

7. What areas of self-discipline will you need to implement to help with the fulfillment of your dream?

Living the Prosperous Life

Living the Prosperous Life

Dear Reader,

I trust that the revelation in this book has opened your understanding to a powerful key for your success and well-being in life. God desires you to live in a continual feast of blessings and steadfast prosperity in every area of your life.

In Genesis 1:27-28, we discover that God created us in His own image, male and female, and He blessed them. You were created to live in the blessing realm. Through Christ, you have been given "every spiritual blessing in the heavenly places" (Ephesians 1:3) and "everything pertaining to life and godliness" (2 Peter 1:3).

Two thousand years ago, Jesus opened the heavens for you and invited you to live a life that is flourishing, succeeding and overflowing with His goodness and blessings. He desires you to prosper in every way all the time. Do you desire this to be made manifest in your life?

God's Law of Attraction is designed to help you live God's abundant life. When you align your soul with His ways, then you will attract the fulfilled will and purpose of God in your life. Determine today to attract God's blessing by filling your soul only with the truth.

My prayer for you is "that in all respects you may prosper and be in good health, just as your soul prospers" (3 John 1:2).

Enjoy the journey into your prosperous future.

BONUS BOOK

Decree

"Decree a thing and it shall be be established."
—Job 22:28

Patricia King

THIRD EDITION

Distributed by:
Patricia King Ministries
P. O. Box 1017
Maricopa, Arizona 85139
PatriciaKing.com

Decree Table of Contents

Introduction

The powerful Word of God is well able to profoundly influence your life. In Christ you have an eternal and unbreakable covenant. All of His promises are *"Yes"* and *"Amen"* (2 Corinthians 1:20) to you! Daily confession of the Word will strengthen your inner man and prepare you for every good work. The following are some reasons why the confession of the Word is found to be powerful in our lives.

The Word of God:

+ Is eternal in the heavens – *Matthew 24:35*
+ Will not return void – *Isaiah 55:11*
+ Frames the will of God – *Hebrews 11:3*
+ Dispatches angels – *Psalm 103:20*
+ Brings light into darkness – *Psalm 119:130*
+ Is a lamp unto our feet and a light unto our path – *Psalm 119:105*
+ Secures blessings – *Ephesians 1:3; 2 Peter 1:3*
+ Is seed – *Mark 4*

- ✦ Is our weapon of warfare – *Ephesians 6:10-20; 2 Corinthians 10:3-5*

- ✦ Pulls down mindsets – *2 Corinthians 10:3-5*

- ✦ Creates – *Romans 4:17*

- ✦ Sanctifies – *John 17:17*

- ✦ Strengthens the spirit man – *Ephesians 5:26*

- ✦ Ensures answers to prayer – *John 15:7*

May you truly enjoy a season of strengthening and may you be forever established in the manifestation of His glorious Word.

In His victorious service with you,

Prayer of Dedication

I dedicate myself to You this day in spirit, soul and body. Convict me of any ways in my thoughts, words or deeds that have been displeasing to You. I ask for cleansing from all sin according to Your Word that promises that if I confess my sin, then You will be faithful to forgive me and to cleanse me from all unrighteousness.

As I confess and decree Your Word, may Your Holy Spirit help me to be a passionate worshipper, a lover of truth, and a faithful child who brings pleasure to Your righteous heart.

May I experience spiritual strengthening through the power of Your Word, for Your Word does not return void but accomplishes everything it is sent to do.

Grant unto me a spirit of wisdom and of revelation in the knowledge of Christ for the glory of Your Name and Kingdom.

In Jesus' name, I pray. AMEN

With my whole heart I have sought You;
Oh, let me not wander from Your
commandments!
Your word I have hidden in my heart,
That I might not sin against You.

— Psalm 119:10-11 —

Praise and Worship

*H*eavenly Father, I worship You in spirit and in truth. Along with the host of heaven, I declare:

Holy, holy, holy, Lord God Almighty,
Who was and is and is to come!
You are worthy, O Lord, to receive glory and honor and power;
For You created all things, and by Your will they exist.
Blessing and honor and glory and power
Be to Him who sits on the throne,
And to the Lamb, forever and ever!
Holy, holy, holy is the Lord of hosts;
The whole earth is full of His glory!

– Revelation 4:8,11; 5:13; Isaiah 6:3

You, O Lord, are sitting on Your throne, high and lifted up, and the train of Your robe fills the temple. I ascribe greatness to You, for You are my God and my Rock. Your work is perfect, and all Your ways are just. You are a God of faithfulness and without injustice; righteous and upright are You.

I love You, O Lord my God, with all my heart, mind and strength. You are the Lord, and there is no other. There is no God besides You. I glory in Your holy name, and my heart rejoices in You. I will seek Your face evermore! I bless You, O Lord, my God. You are very great. You are clothed with honor and majesty.

While I live, I will praise You. I will sing praises to You while I have my being. The high praises of God will be in my mouth and a two-edged sword in my hand.

> *Praise the Lord!*
> *Praise the Lord from the heavens;*
> *Praise Him in the heights!*
> *Praise Him, all His angels;*
> *Praise Him, all His hosts!*
> *Praise Him, sun and moon;*
> *Praise Him, all you stars of light!*
> *Praise Him, you heavens of heavens,*
> *And you waters above the heavens!*
> *— Psalm 148:1-4*

Scriptural References:
Deuteronomy 32:3-4; Psalm 104:1; 105:3-4; 146:2; 149:6; Isaiah 6:1; 45:5; John 4:24

Everlasting Love

The Lord loves me with an everlasting love and has promised to give me a future and a hope. With lovingkindness He has drawn me unto Himself. I look carefully and intently at the manner of love the Father has poured out upon me. It is through this love that He has called me to be His dear child. I am completely and fully accepted in Him, my God and Savior.

Nothing can separate me from the love of God that is in Christ Jesus my Lord – not tribulation or distress, not persecution, famine or nakedness; not peril, sword, angels, principalities, powers; death, nor life; neither things present nor things to come – absolutely nothing can separate me from the love of God which is in Christ Jesus my Lord.

God's love towards me is patient and kind. His love for me bears all things, believes all things, hopes all things and endures all things. His love will never fail. His love for me is so rich that He gave His only begotten Son. Because of this, I will never perish but will have everlasting life with Him. As a result of God's great love for me, I have an unbreakable, eternal covenant with Him. Through this covenant of love, He has put His laws within my heart and has written His commandments upon my mind.

I have been invited to the Lord's banqueting table and His banner over me is love! His love is better than the choicest of wines.

Through His intimate love, He draws and invites me to follow after Him. I am fair and pleasant unto Him. I am rooted and grounded in His love and am well able to comprehend with all believers what is the width and length and depth and height of His unfailing love. I have been called to know this rich love that surpasses knowledge so that I may be filled with all the fullness of God. I truly am the object of His deepest love and affection!

Christ's perfect love has cast out fear in me and has enabled me to be a passionate lover of God and others. Love is my greatest aim in life.

Scriptural References:
Song of Solomon 1:2,4; 2:4; Jeremiah 31:3; Matthew 22:37-40; John 3:16; Romans 8:38-39; 1 Corinthians 13:4,7-8; 14:1; Ephesians 1:6,18-19; Hebrews 8:10; 1

Who I Am in Christ

I am a child of God; God is spiritually my Father.
Romans 8:14-15; Galatians 3:26; 4:6; John 1:12

I am a new creation in Christ; old things have passed away and all things have become new.
2 Corinthians 5:17

I am in Christ.
Ephesians 1:1-4; Galatians 3:26,28

I am an heir with the Father and a joint heir with Christ.
Galatians 4:6-7; Romans 8:17

I am reconciled to God and am an ambassador of reconciliation for Him.
2 Corinthians 5:18-19

I am a saint.
Ephesians 1:1; 1 Corinthians 1:2; Philippians 1:1; Colossians 1:2

I am God's workmanship, created in Christ for good works.
Ephesians 2:10

I am a citizen of heaven.
Ephesians 2:19; Philippians 3:20

I am a member of Christ's body.
1 Corinthians 12:27

I am united to the Lord and am one spirit with Him.
1 Corinthians 6:17

I am the temple of the Holy Spirit.
1 Corinthians 3:16; 6:19

I am a friend of Christ.
John 15:15

I am a slave of righteousness.
Romans 6:18

I am the righteousness of God in Christ.
2 Corinthians 5:21

I am enslaved to God.
Romans 6:22

I am chosen and ordained by Christ to bear fruit.
John 15:16

I am a prisoner of Christ.
Ephesians 3:1; 4:1

I am righteous and holy.
Ephesians 4:24

I am hidden with Christ in God.
Colossians 3:3

I am the salt of the earth.
Matthew 5:13

I am the light of the world.
Matthew 5:14

I am part of the true vine.
John 15:1-2

I am filled with the divine nature of Christ and escape the corruption that is in the world through lust.
2 Peter 1:4

I am an expression of the life of Christ.
Colossians 3:4

I am chosen of God, holy and dearly loved.
Colossians 3:12; 1 Thessalonians 1:4

I am a child of light.
1 Thessalonians 5:5

I am a partaker of a heavenly calling.
Hebrews 3:1

I am more than a conqueror through Christ.
Romans 8:37

I am a partaker with Christ and share in His life.
Hebrews 3:14

I am one of God's living stones, being built up in Christ as a spiritual house.
1 Peter 2:5

I am a chosen generation, a royal priesthood, a holy nation.
1 Peter 2:9

I am the devil's enemy.
1 Peter 5:8

I am born again by the Spirit of God.
John 3:3-6

I am an alien and stranger to this world.
1 Peter 2:11

I am a child of God who always triumphs in Christ and releases His fragrance in every place.
2 Corinthians 2:14

I am seated in heavenly places in Christ.
Ephesians 2:6

I am saved by grace.
Ephesians 2:8

I am a recipient of every spiritual blessing in the heavenly places in Christ.
Ephesians 1:3

I am redeemed by the blood of the Lamb.
Revelation 5:9

I am part of the bride of Christ and am making myself ready for Him.
Revelation 19:7

I am a true worshipper who worships the Father in spirit and in truth.
John 4:24

Blessing

I am created for blessing. As a result, I am fruitful in every good thing and I multiply and increase in blessing. Because my God has blessed me, no curse can touch me. In the name of Jesus Christ and by the power of His blood, I decree His covenant of blessing around my life and all that pertains to me.

Nothing but blessing is permitted to come into my life or sphere of influence. If the enemy attempts to attack me, he will be caught in the act and pay sevenfold what he stole and then I will plunder his house, for I only accept blessing. His attempts create testimonies of God's increased blessings in my life.

Like Abraham, I am blessed and am called to be a blessing. Through my life in Jesus, nations are blessed.

Blessings come upon me and overtake me. Blessings are attracted to me. I am a blessing magnet. I am blessed coming in and blessed going out. I am blessed in the city and blessed in the field. The heavens are open over my life and the rain of God's abundant goodness falls on my life and all that pertains to me. No good thing has He withheld from me. I am blessed in everything I put my hands to.

My household is blessed. My food is blessed. My clothing is blessed. My vehicles are blessed. My business and matters of business are blessed. My children, family, and all who labor with me and for me are blessed. My finances are blessed and my spirit, soul, and body are fully blessed, because Jesus established an eternal, unbreakable covenant of blessing for me.

I am blessed with the Kingdom of heaven and its bounty because I recognize my need of God in all things and at all times. I am blessed with comfort when I mourn. I am always blessed with a satisfied heart because I hunger and thirst for righteousness. I am blessed with mercy because I show mercy to others. I am blessed with insights and visitations from God because I am pure in spirit.

I am called a son/daughter of God because I am a peacemaker. When I am persecuted for the sake of righteousness or when people insult me and speak lies about me, I am blessed with heavenly and eternal reward. I am blessed because I hear the Lord's Word and act on it. I am a doer of the Word and not a hearer only.

Because I love wisdom and righteousness I am blessed and my dwelling is blessed. The blessing of the Lord has made me rich and He adds no sorrow to it. Because I trust in the Lord I am blessed. I am blessed with every spiritual blessing in the heavenly places in Christ. Grace and peace are multiplied unto me in the knowledge of Christ.

I have been granted everything that pertains to life and to godliness. I have been given all the magnificent promises in the Word of God. I sow blessings bountifully and therefore I reap blessings bountifully. I always look for ways I can bless others. The Lord blesses me, indeed, and enlarges my realms of influence. His hand of grace and blessing is with me, and He keeps me from harm. I am truly blessed in all things, for my Father in heaven has chosen gladly to give me the Kingdom.

My God blesses me continuously and causes His face to shine upon
me. He is gracious unto me and grants me peace.

Scriptural References:
*Genesis 1:28; 12:2; Deuteronomy 28:1-13; Numbers 6:22-27;
Proverbs 3:13,33; 6:31; 10:6; 10:22; 16:20; Matthew 5:3-11;
Luke 11:28; 12:32; Ephesians 1:3; 2 Peter 1:2-4; James 1:22;
1 Chronicles 4:10*

Favor

*I*n Christ Jesus, I am favored by my heavenly Father. The favor He has given His Son has been given to me. This is undeserved, unmerited favor that is granted me in Christ. His favor is a free gift to me, for which I am very thankful. As Jesus kept increasing in wisdom and stature, and in favor with God and men, so also do I, because I abide in Jesus and He abides in me.

I embrace the favor of God, for it is better than silver and gold. The favor of God on my life endures for a lifetime and causes my mountain of influence and blessing to stand strong. His favor surrounds me like a shield against my enemies.

The Lord favors me with vindication and delights in my prosperity. His blessing on my life attracts the rich among the people who seek my favor.

By the favor of the Lord, the works of my hands are confirmed and established. All that I put my hands to is favored. My steps are bathed in butter and the rock pours out oil for me. As I seek the Lord's favor, He is gracious unto me according to His Word. I am favored in my home and favored in the workplace. I am favored everywhere I go and in all that I do.

I love wisdom and seek diligently for wisdom and understanding. Therefore I have been granted favor by the Lord and am favored by others. In the light of my King's face is life, and His favor is like a cloud with the spring rain over me. His favor is like heavenly dew that falls on my life.

I am favored in His presence and He goes before me revealing His goodness and glory to me. His favor opens doors of opportunity for me that no man can shut. By His favor I have been granted the keys of the Kingdom and whatever I bind on earth is bound in heaven. Whatever I loose on earth has been loosed in heaven. His righteous scepter of favor is extended towards me. Whatever I ask in the name of Christ He grants unto me when I make my requests and petitions according to His will. He daily grants me great favor because of the covenant blood of Christ and the promises in His Word.

Blessed be the Lord who favors His people!

Scriptural References:
Exodus 33:13-19; Esther 5:2; Job 29:6; Psalm 5:12; 30:5,7; 45:6,12; 90:17; 119:58; Proverbs 8:35; 11:27; 16:15; 19:12; 22:1; Isaiah 45:1; Luke 2:52; John 15:7 17:22

Victory

I am a child of the living God. I am an heir of God and a joint heir with Jesus Christ. I am a new creation in Jesus and old things have passed away and all things have become new. I am a chosen generation, a royal priesthood, a holy nation.

I am not under guilt or condemnation. I refuse discouragement because it is not of God. God is the God of all encouragement. There is therefore now no condemnation for those who are in Christ Jesus. The law of the Spirit of life in Christ Jesus has set me free from the law of sin and death. I do not listen to Satan's accusations, for he is a liar, the father of lies. I gird up my loins with truth. Sin does not have dominion over me.

I flee from temptation, but if I do sin I have an advocate with the Father who is Jesus Christ. I confess my sins and forsake them. God is faithful and just to forgive me, cleansing me from all unrighteousness. I am cleansed by the blood of the Lamb. I am an overcomer because of the blood of Jesus and because of the word of my testimony.

No weapon that is formed against me shall prosper and I shall confute every tongue that rises up against me in judgment. My mind is renewed by the Word of God.

The weapons of my warfare are not carnal but mighty through God to the pulling down of strongholds; I cast down imaginations and every high thing that exalts itself against the knowledge of Christ. I bring every thought captive into obedience to the truth.

I am accepted in the Beloved. Greater is He that is in me than he that is in the world. Nothing can separate me from the love of God which is in Christ Jesus my Lord. I am the righteousness of God in Christ Jesus. I am not the slave of sin but of righteousness. I continue in His Word. I know the truth and the truth sets me free. Because Christ has set me free, I am free indeed. I have been delivered out of the domain of darkness and am now abiding in the Kingdom of God.

I am not intimidated by the enemy's lies. He is defeated. For this purpose Christ came into the world, to destroy the works of the evil one. I submit to God and resist the devil. The enemy flees from me in terror because the Lord lives mightily in me. I give the devil no opportunity. I give no place to fear in my life. God has not given me a spirit of fear but of love, of power and of a sound mind. Terror shall not come near me because the Lord is the strength of my life and He always causes me to triumph in Christ Jesus.

In Christ, I am the head and not the tail. I am above and not beneath. A thousand shall fall at my side and ten thousand at my right hand, and none shall touch me. I am seated with Christ in the heavenly places far above all principalities and powers. I have been given power to tread upon serpents, scorpions and over all the power of the enemy. Nothing shall injure me. No longer will the enemy oppress me. I defeat him by the authority that Christ has given me. I am more than a conqueror through Christ.

Scriptural References:
Deuteronomy 28:13; Psalm 27:1; 91:7; Isaiah 54:17; Luke 10:19;

John 8:36,44; Romans 6:16; 8:1-2,17,32,37,39; 12:2; 2 Corinthians 2:14; 5:17,21; 10:3-5; Ephesians 1:6,20-21; 4:27; 6:14; Colossians 1:13; 2 Timothy 1:7; James 4:7; 1 Peter 2:9; 1 John 1:9; 2:1; 3:8; Revelation 12:11

Wisdom

Jesus Christ has become wisdom, righteousness, sanctification and redemption unto me. Because Christ dwells within me, I know wisdom and instruction. My God gives unto me a spirit of wisdom and of revelation in the knowledge of Christ. When I lack wisdom, I ask in faith and it is given to me generously. This is heavenly wisdom which is first pure, then peaceable, gentle, easily entreated, full of mercy and good fruits, unwavering and without hypocrisy.

I discern the sayings of understanding and I receive instruction in wise behavior, justice and fairness. I walk in the fear of the Lord which is the beginning of knowledge. Jesus pours out His spirit of wisdom upon me and makes His words of wisdom known to me.

I receive the sayings of wisdom and I treasure the com-mandments of the Lord within me. My ear is attentive to wisdom and I incline my heart to understanding. I cry for discernment and lift my voice for understanding. I seek for wisdom as for silver and search for it as for hidden treasures. Because of this I will discern the fear of the Lord and discover the knowledge of God. The Lord gives me wisdom.

From His mouth comes knowledge and understanding. He stores up sound wisdom for me. He is a shield to me. He guards my paths with justice and preserves my way. Wisdom enters my heart and knowledge is pleasant to my soul. Discretion guards me and understanding watches over me to deliver me from the way of evil.

I do not let kindness and truth leave me. I bind them around my neck and write them on the tablet of my heart so that I find favor and good repute with God and man. I trust in the Lord with all my heart and I do not lean on my own understanding. In all my ways I acknowledge Him and He makes my paths straight. I am blessed because I find wisdom and I gain understanding.

I have a long, full life because it is in wisdom's right hand, and I have the riches and honor that are in wisdom's left hand. Because I love wisdom, all my paths are peace and my ways pleasant. Wisdom is a tree of life to me and I am blessed because I hold her fast. I inherit honor because of my love for wisdom, and my dwelling is blessed.

I acquire wisdom and understanding. I do not forsake wisdom; therefore, wisdom is my guard. I love wisdom and am watched over. Because I prize and embrace wisdom, wisdom exalts and honors me. Wisdom places a garland of grace on my head and presents me with a crown of beauty. I call wisdom my sister and understanding my intimate friend.

Because I love wisdom, both riches and honor are with me, enduring wealth and righteousness. Wisdom endows me with wealth and fills my treasuries. I listen to wisdom and daily watch at her gates. I eat wisdom's food and drink of the wine that she has mixed. I forsake folly and live. I proceed in the way of understanding. When I speak, I speak noble things, and the opening of my mouth produces right things. My mouth utters truth. All the utterances of my mouth are in righteousness because I walk in the way of wisdom.

Scriptural References:
Proverbs 1:2-3,7,23; 2:1-12; 4:5-9; 7:4; 8:6-8; 9:5-6;
1 Corinthians 1:30; Ephesians 1:17; James 1:5; 3:17

Glory

In Christ I am filled with and have access to the same glory the Father gave to His Son. Jesus is a shield to me each and every day. He is the glory and the lifter of my head.

Jesus is the King of glory and He lives powerfully in me because I open up the gates of my heart and life to Him. He is the Lord of hosts who is strong and mighty. He is mighty in all my battles. Jesus, the King of glory, prevails over all my enemies. His glory is my rear guard and my back is always covered. When I am persecuted for the sake of righteousness, I am greatly rewarded because the spirit of glory and of God rests upon me. In Christ, I inherit the throne of glory. I am seated with Him in the heavenly places far above all demonic forces and dominions.

The fire of the Lord surrounds me and He is glory in the midst of me. The glory of His presence goes before me at all times and gives me rest. His glory is manifest in His great goodness that visits my life each day. I decree, "The Lord is good and His lovingkindness endures forever! The Lord is good and His lovingkindness endures forever!" As I make this sure confession, the glory of the Lord fills my body, His temple, afresh.

I arise and shine because Jesus, my Light, has come, and the glory of the Lord has risen upon me. In the midst of great darkness that covers the earth, the glory appears upon me. Nations and kings come to the brightness of my rising.

I have access to the wealth, gold and silver in the earth as a result of the glory of Christ that is in me and on me. All the gold and all the silver is His. All the earth and its fullness belong to Him and all that is His has been given to me in Christ. I exercise my faith to receive the fullness of His glory and, as a result, the latter glory of the house (my life) is greater than the former.

All my needs are met according to His riches in glory by Christ Jesus. The knowledge of His glory – the glory of His salvation, healing, deliverance, provision, strength, signs and wonders, and presence – fills the earth as the waters cover the sea. The Lord's works appear to me and His glory to my children.

Glory and honor are in His presence. Strength and gladness are in His place. I imbibe of His goodness each and every day and declare His glory and marvelous works.

Be exalted, O God, above the heavens. Let your glory be above all the earth. In You my salvation and glory rest. Blessed be the name of the Lord forever, and may the whole earth be filled with Your glory. Amen and Amen.

Scriptural References:
Exodus 33:14-19; 1 Samuel 2:8; 1 Chronicles 16:24,27; Psalm 3:3; 24:1,7-10; 57:11; 62:7; 72:19; 90:16; 96:3; Isaiah 58:8; 60:1-3,5,9; Habakkuk 2:14; Haggai 2:8-9; Zechariah 2:5; John 17:22; Ephesians 1:20-22, 2:6; Philippians 4:19; 1 Peter 4:14

Provision and Resource

I seek first the Kingdom of God and His righteousness, and all the things that I need are added unto me, for my heavenly Father knows what I need even before I ask. I do not fear, for it is my Father's good pleasure to give me the Kingdom.

I acknowledge that all my needs are met according to God's riches in glory by Christ Jesus. Grace and peace are multiplied unto me through the knowledge of God and of Jesus my Lord. His divine power has given me all things that pertain unto life and godliness, through the knowledge of Him who has called me to glory and virtue. Blessed be the God and Father of my Lord Jesus Christ, who has blessed me with every spiritual blessing in the heavenly places in Christ. The Lord is a sun and a shield to me and will give me grace and glory. No good thing will He withhold from me as I walk uprightly.

I choose to sow bountifully, therefore I will reap bountifully. I give to the Lord, to His people, and to the needy as I purpose in my heart to give. I do not give grudgingly or out of compulsion, for my God loves a cheerful giver. God makes all grace abound towards me, that I always have enough for all things so that I may abound unto every good work.

The Lord supplies seed for me to sow and bread for my food. He also supplies and multiplies my seed for sowing, and He increases the fruits of my righteousness. I am enriched in everything unto great abundance, which brings much thanksgiving to God.

I bring all my tithes into the Lord's storehouse so that there is meat in His house. As a result, He opens up the windows of heaven and pours out a blessing for me so that there is not room enough to contain it. He rebukes the devourer for my sake, so that he does not destroy the fruits of my ground and neither does my vine cast its grapes before the time. All the nations shall call me blessed for I shall have a delightful life. I am blessed because I consider the poor. Because I give freely to the poor, I will never want. My righteousness endures forever.

I remember the Lord my God, for it is He who gives me the power to make wealth, that He may confirm His covenant. Because Jesus Christ, my Savior, diligently listened to the voice of God and obeyed all the commandments, the Lord will set me high above all the nations of the earth, and all the blessings in the Kingdom shall come upon me and overtake me. Christ became poor so that through His poverty I might become rich.

The Lord increases me a thousand-fold more than I am, and blesses me just as He has promised. He prospers everything I put my hand to. I abound in prosperity. The Lord empowers me to work provisional miracles in His name. I witness miracles of multiplication, debt cancellation, and increase. Jesus came so that I would have life in its abundance. I am very blessed and favored of God and have been called to be a blessing to others.

Scriptural References
Genesis 12:2; Deuteronomy 1:11; 8:18; 28:1-2, 11-12; 1 Kings 17:9-16; 2 Kings 4:1-7; Psalm 41:1; 84:11; 112:1,9; Proverbs 28:27; Malachi 3:8-12; Matthew 6:33; Mark 6:33-44; Luke 12:32; John 10:10; 2 Corinthians 8:9; 9:6-11; Ephesians 1:3; Philippians 4:19; 2 Peter 1:2-3

Christian Character

I am the light of the world. A city set on a hill cannot be hid. I let my light so shine before men that they may see my good works and glorify my Father which is in heaven. Grace and peace are multiplied to me through the knowledge of God and of Jesus my Lord. His divine power has granted me everything that pertains to life and to godliness.

He has given me exceeding great and precious promises. I live by these promises so that I might partake of His divine nature, having escaped the corruption that is in the world through lust. Besides this, I give all diligence and add to my faith virtue, to virtue knowledge, to knowledge temperance, to temperance patience, and to patience godliness. To godliness I add brotherly kindness, to brotherly kindness love. As these things are in me and abounding, I shall never be barren nor unfruitful in the knowledge of my Lord Jesus.

I choose to walk worthy of the Lord in every respect, being fruitful in every good work and increasing in the knowledge of God. I give thanks to my heavenly Father who has made me to be a partaker of the inheritance of the saints in light. He has delivered me from the power of darkness and has translated me to the Kingdom of His dear Son in whom I have redemption through His blood, even the forgiveness of sin.

I am an imitator of God as a dear child. I walk in love. Covetousness, fornication and all uncleanness have no part in my life, neither filthiness nor coarse jesting, nor foolish talking, which are not fitting, but rather the giving of thanks. I let no corrupt communication proceed out of my mouth, but only that which is good to the use of edifying, that it may minister grace to the hearers. I will not grieve the Holy Spirit of God whereby I have been sealed unto the day of redemption.

I choose to walk in lowliness of mind and esteem others as better than myself. I look not to my own interests but also to the interests of others. I make myself of no reputation and take the form of a bondservant.

I wait for the Lord and let integrity and uprightness preserve me. Jesus is a buckler to me because I walk uprightly. I dwell on those things that are true and honorable, whatever is right, whatever is pure, whatever is lovely, whatever is of good repute and anything that is excellent and worthy of praise.

As a child of God, I am thoroughly furnished for every good work. I consider how to provoke others to love. I put on a heart of compassion, kindness, humility, gentleness and patience. I am God's workmanship, created in Christ Jesus for good deeds which God prepared beforehand that I should walk in them.

I am patient and kind. I am not jealous. I do not brag and I am not arrogant. I do not act unbecomingly and do not seek my own way. I am not easily provoked and do not take into account a wrong suffered. I do not rejoice in unrighteousness, but rejoice with the truth. I bear all things, believe all things, hope all things and endure all things. The love of Jesus in me does not fail.

Scriptural References:
Matthew 5:14-16; 1 Corinthians 13:4-8; Ephesians 2:10; 4:29-30; 5:1-5; Philippians 2:3-7; 4:8; Colossians 1:9-14; 3:12; 2 Peter 1:2-8; Hebrews 10:24; 2 Timothy 3:17

Spiritual Strength

I am strong in the Lord and in the strength of His might. I put on the full armor of God. In Christ I can do all things because He strengthens me.

The Lord is my strength and my shield; my heart trusts in Him, and I am helped; therefore my heart exults and with my song I shall thank Him. He is my strength and my saving defense in time of trouble. The grace of the Lord Jesus Christ is with my spirit.

I build myself up in my holy faith, praying in the Holy Spirit. As I do this, I keep myself strong in the love of God. My God keeps me from falling and presents me faultless and blameless in the presence of my heavenly Father with exceeding great joy.

My help comes from the Lord who made heaven and earth. He will not allow my foot to slip and He who keeps me will not slumber. The Lord is my keeper. The Lord is my shade on my right hand. The sun does not smite me by day nor the moon by night. The Lord protects me from all evil. He keeps my soul and He guards my going out and my coming in from this time forth and forever.

When I pass through the valley of weeping, the Lord makes it a spring for me. I go from strength to strength in the Lord. The Lord God is a sun and a shield to me. He gives me grace and glory, and no good thing does He withhold from me. I am blessed because I trust in Him.

My heavenly Father grants unto me according to the riches of His glory the ability to be strengthened with power through His Spirit in my inner man, so that Christ may dwell in my heart through faith, and that I, being rooted and grounded in love, may be able to comprehend with all believers what is the breadth and length and height and depth and to know the love of Christ which surpasses knowledge, that I may be filled up to all the fullness of God.

I do not lose heart in doing good, for in due time I shall reap if I faint not. My eye is single, therefore my whole being is full of light. I am steadfast, immoveable, always abounding in the work of the Lord, knowing that my toil is not in vain in the Lord. God is my strong fortress and He sets me in His way.

By Him, I can run through a troop and by my God, I can leap over a wall. He is a shield because I take refuge in Him. He makes my feet like hinds' feet and sets me on my high places. He trains my hands for battle so that my arms can bend a bow of bronze. He has given me the shield of His salvation and His help and strength make me great. I pursue my enemies and destroy them because the Lord has girded me with strength for battle.

The Lord gives me strength when I am weary, and when I lack might He increases power. I wait on the Lord and renew my strength. I mount up with wings like eagles. I run and do not get tired; I walk and do not faint.

Scriptural References:
2 Samuel 22:30-40; Psalm 28:7-8; 37:39; 84:5-7,11; 121:1-8; Isaiah 40:29-31; Matthew 6:22; 1 Corinthians 15:58; Galatians 6:7-9; Ephesians 3:16-19; 6:10; Philippians 4:13,23; Jude 20-21,24

Empowered to Go

I receive power when the Holy Spirit comes upon me to be the Lord's witness even unto the uttermost parts of the earth. In Jesus' name I go into all the world to preach the gospel to every creature.

These signs follow me as I go because I believe. In the name of Jesus, I cast out devils, I speak with new tongues, I take up serpents, and if I drink any deadly poison it shall not harm me. When I lay hands on the sick they shall recover. I go forth and preach everywhere, and the Lord confirms the Word I preach with signs that follow. When I go, I go in the fullness of the blessing of the gospel of Christ.

The works that Jesus does, I do also in His name and even greater works I do because He has gone to the Father. Greater is He that is in me than he that is in the world. Jesus has given me power over all the power of the enemy. He has given me power over unclean spirits to cast them out and has enabled me to heal all manner of sickness and all manner of disease.

As I go, I will preach saying, "The kingdom of heaven is at hand." I will heal the sick, cleanse the lepers, raise the dead. I will cast out devils, because freely I have received so I will freely give. The Lord grants me boldness to speak His Word. He stretches out His hand toward me to heal, that signs and wonders may be done through the name of Jesus Christ. His Spirit has been poured out upon me and I prophesy.

All power in heaven and in earth has been given unto Jesus Christ. I will go in His name and teach all nations, baptizing them in the name of the Father, the Son and the Holy Spirit. I will teach them to observe all things that Jesus has taught me. Jesus is with me even unto the end of the world. He has called me to Himself and has given me power and authority over all devils and to cure diseases. He has sent me to preach the Kingdom of God and to heal the sick. As I go, Jesus prepares my way with His favor, for the Lord surrounds His righteous with favor as a shield. He sends His angels before me to watch over my ways and to bear me up lest I fall.

Like Jesus, I have been anointed with the Holy Spirit and with power. I go about doing good and healing all that are oppressed of the devil, for God is with me. He has anointed me to preach the gospel to the poor. He has sent me to proclaim release to the captives and recovery of sight to the blind, to set free all who are downtrodden, and to proclaim the favorable year of the Lord.

I arise and shine because my light has come and the glory of the Lord has risen upon me. Darkness shall cover the earth and gross darkness the peoples, but the Lord has risen upon me and His glory appears upon me. Nations will come to my light in Christ and kings to the brightness of my rising.

My speech and my preaching is not with enticing words of man's wisdom. It is in the demonstration of the Spirit and of power that the faith of those I preach to should not stand on the wisdom of men but in the power of God, for the Kingdom of God is not in word but in power.

The Lord grants unto me, according to His riches in glory, to be strengthened with might by His Spirit in my inner man according to His glorious power unto all patience and longsuffering with joy. I labor according to His power that works mightily within me.

I preach not myself, but Christ Jesus as Lord, and myself as a bond-servant of Christ and His body for Jesus' sake. For God, who said that "Light shall shine out of darkness," is the One who has shone in our hearts to give the light of the knowledge of the glory of God in the face of Christ. I have this treasure in an earthen vessel, that the surpassing greatness of the power may be of God and not of myself.

Now unto the King eternal, immortal, invisible, the only wise God who is able to do exceedingly, abundantly above all that I could ask or think, according to the power that works within me, be honor and glory forever and ever. AMEN

Scriptural References:
Psalm 5:12; 91:11; Isaiah 60:1-3; Matthew 10:1,7; 28:18-20; Mark 16:15-21; Luke 4:18; 10:1-2,19; John 14:12; Acts 1:8; 2:17-18; 4:29-30; 10:38; Romans 15:29; 1 Corinthians 2:4; 4:19; 2 Corinthians 4:5-6; Ephesians 3:16,20; Colossians 1:11,29; 1 Timothy 1:17; 1 John 4:4

Health and Healing

I praise the Lord with all that is within me and do not forget any of His benefits. He forgives all my sins and heals all my diseases; He redeems my life from the pit and crowns me with love and compassion. Jesus satisfies my desires with good things so that my youth is renewed like the eagle's.

The Lord brings me to health and healing. He heals me and lets me enjoy abundant peace and security. The Sun of Righteousness arises for me with healing in His wings and I go out and leap like a calf released from the stall. Jesus bore my sins in His body on the cross so that I might die to sin and live to righteousness. By His stripes I am healed. As my days are, so shall my strength be.

Jesus sent forth His Word and healed me; He rescued me from the grave. When I cry out, the Lord hears me; He delivers me from all my troubles. The Lord is close to me when I am brokenhearted and saves me when I am crushed in spirit. He has not given me a spirit of fear but of love, power and a sound mind.

At times I may have many troubles, but the Lord delivers me from them all; He protects all my bones; not one of them will be broken. I am like an olive tree flourishing in the house of God; I trust in God's unfailing love forever and ever.

When the Lord's servants lay hands on me I recover and when I am sick I call for the elders who pray over me, anointing me with oil in the name of the Lord. The prayer of faith saves me and the Lord raises me up.

The law of the spirit of life in Christ Jesus has set me free from the law of sin and death. Jesus is the resurrection and the life. Because I believe in Him, I will live for all eternity. In Christ I live and move and have my being.

Because I dwell in the shelter of the Most High and rest in the shadow of the Almighty, I will say of the Lord, "He is my refuge and my fortress, my God, in whom I trust." Surely He will save me from the fowler's snare and from the deadly pestilence. He covers me with His feathers, and under His wings I find refuge; His faithfulness is my shield and rampart. I do not fear the terror of night, nor the arrow that flies by day, nor the pestilence that stalks in the darkness, nor the plague that destroys at midday. A thousand may fall at my side, ten thousand at my right hand, but they will not come near me. I will only observe with my eyes and see the punishment of the wicked. Because I make the Most High my dwelling – even the Lord, who is my refuge – then no harm will befall me, no disaster will come near my tent. He will command His angels concerning me to guard me in all my ways; they will lift me up in their hands so I will not strike my foot against a stone. I will tread upon the lion and the cobra; I will trample the great lion and the serpent. Because I love the Lord, He will rescue and protect me from all accident, harm, sickness and disease. He is with me in trouble and delivers me. With long life He satisfies me and shows me His salvation.

Because I consider the poor, the Lord will deliver me in time of trouble. The Lord will protect me and keep me alive, and I shall be blessed upon the earth. He will not give me over to the desire of my enemies. The Lord will sustain me upon my sickbed; in my illness, He will restore me to health.

Scriptural References:
Deuteronomy 33:25; Psalm 34:17-20; 41:1-3; 52:8; 91; 103:1-3; 107:20; Jeremiah 33:6; Malachi 4:2; Mark 16:18; John 11:25-26; Romans 12:1; 2 Timothy 1:7; James 5:14-15; 1 Peter 2:24

Business, Ministry, and Workplace

*I*n my business, ministry, and workplace I am surrounded with favor as a shield. I arise and shine, for my light has come. The rich among the people entreat my favor.

In Christ I show no defect but function in intelligence in every branch of wisdom, being endowed with understanding and discerning knowledge. The Lord gives me the knowledge of witty inventions and causes me to grow in wisdom, in stature, and in favor with God and man.

In my business, ministry, and workplace, I am the head and not the tail. I am above and not beneath. The Lord commands blessings upon my business, ministry, and workplace, and every project that I put my hands to prospers. He establishes my business, ministry, and workplace as holy unto Himself.

My business, ministry, and workplace do not submit to the Babylonian/world system, but instead submit to the Kingdom of God and His righteousness. The integrity of the Lord guides me in my business. The Lord leans upon my business, ministry, and workplace with regard and makes it fruitful, multiplying its productivity.

No weapon formed against my business, ministry, and workplace prospers. Every tongue that rises up against it in judgement I condemn, and the Lord vindicates me. The Lord is a wall of fire around my business and workplace, and His glory is in the midst of it.

The Lord leads me by His presence, and He gives me rest. He makes goodness to pass before my business, ministry, and workplace. His goodness and mercy follow me all the days of my life. Peace, unity, love, integrity, honor, and servanthood are godly values that prevail in my business, ministry, and workplace.

I decree that Jesus Christ is Lord over my life, business, ministry, and workplace!

Scriptural References:
Exodus 33:14,19; Leviticus 26:9; Deuteronomy 28:1-13; Psalm 5:12; 23:6; 45:12; Proverbs 11:3; Isaiah 54:17; 60:1; Daniel 1:4; Zechariah 2:5; Revelation 18:4

Family and Children

As for me and my family, we will serve the Lord. Because I believe in the Lord Jesus Christ, I shall be saved, and my entire house. Because I am a covenant child of God, my household is blessed. We have been blessed with every spiritual blessing in Christ. Blessings come upon us and overtake us.

My family, home, marriage, and children are blessed, and all that I put my hands to do. I am blessed coming in and I am blessed going out. The Lord has established my household as a people for Himself. He causes us to abound in prosperity in the offspring of our bodies, in the offspring of our beasts, and in the produce of our ground. The Lord surrounds my family and entire household with favor as a shield. No good thing does He withhold from us. His banner is love over my home, marriage, and family. No weapon formed against us as a family prospers. What the Lord has blessed, no man can curse. We abide in the shadow of the Almighty and no evil befalls us.

My children shall be mighty on the earth, for the generation of the upright are blessed. They shall be as signs and wonders in the earth.

My children will flourish like olive plants around my table. They are a gift from the Lord, and the fruit of the womb is my reward. My children are like arrows in the hand of a warrior. My sons in their youth are as grown-up plants and my daughters as corner pillars fashioned as for a palace.

Lord, Your covenant with me declares that Your Spirit which is upon me and Your words which You have put in my mouth shall not depart from my mouth, nor from the mouths of my children, nor from the mouths of my children's children. All my children shall be taught of the Lord, and great shall be their peace and prosperity. In righteousness they will be established and they will be far from oppression. They will not be led into temptation but they will know deliverance from evil.

I confess that my children are pure in heart and therefore they shall see God. They hunger and thirst after righteousness, therefore they are filled. The Spirit of the Lord is poured out upon my children and they prophesy. The Lord's blessing is upon them. They will spring up among the grass like poplars by streams of water. One will say, I am the Lord's, and another one will call on the name of Jacob; and another will write on their hand, "Belonging to the Lord."

I confess that my children are seekers of wisdom and understanding. They hold fast to Your Word and to Your ways. They treasure Your commandments and they cry for discernment. The spirit of wisdom is poured out upon my children and my children's children, and words of wisdom are being made known to them.

The Lord keeps my family from falling and presents them blameless before the presence of the Father's glory with exceeding joy.

Scriptural References:
Deuteronomy 28:1-12; Joshua 24:15; Psalm 5:12; 84:11; 91:1,10; 112:2; 127:3-4; 128:3; 144:12; Proverbs 1:23; 2:2-3; Song of Solomon 2:4; Isaiah 8:18; 44:3-5; 54:13-14,17; 59:21; Matthew 5:6,8; 6:13; Acts 2:17; 16:31; Ephesians 1:3; Jude 24

Great Grace

*G*reat grace abundantly blesses me, fills me, and empowers me each and every day. God's grace (His undeserved, unmerited favor toward me and His divine influence upon my heart and life) enables me to fulfill His will and purpose in and through my life.

The grace of the Lord Jesus Christ is at work within me both to will and to do of His good pleasure.

I am saved by grace, justified by grace, and enabled to fulfill His daily work by His amazing grace. His grace and peace are multiplied unto me as I humble myself before Him. As I increase in grace and power, I will perform wonders and signs among the people that will bring glory to God.

I have been granted grace by Christ to enable me to walk in the gifts and callings I was destined to fulfill. Jesus has invited me to come boldly before His throne of grace so that I may obtain mercy and grace to help in time of trouble. I have free access to this glorious privilege through the blood of Christ.

I am not under the law or in bondage to it, but I enjoy the grace of God who fulfilled all the law for me through Christ. I have the fulfillment of the law within me because of the finished work of the Cross. God's amazing grace has granted me everything that pertains to life and to godliness. I have done nothing to deserve this good-ness and favor, as it is a gift given because of His great love for me.

I choose to live worthy of the grace of God. I allow His grace to motivate me to do His will and purposes and to enable me to bring glory to His name. God's grace teaches me to live a godly life and to deny sin. His grace grants me a heart that desires and loves righ-teousness. As a result, I love righteousness and hate wickedness and am anointed with the oil of joy in great measure.

The grace of my Lord Jesus Christ grants me favor and success every-where I go and in all that I do as I follow Him. As grace has been extended toward me, I extend grace to others and therefore show them the goodness and love of God. Freely, freely, I have received, so I freely, freely give.

Today, I receive increased and multiplied measures of His amazing grace. I am forever grateful to God for His glorious gift of amazing grace and therefore I proclaim His grace and peace to others.

Scripture References:
Matthew 10:8; John 1:16; Acts 15:11; Romans 6:7; Ephesians 1:2; 2:5-8; Philippians 2:13; 2 Timothy 1:9; Hebrews 4:16; James 4:6; 2 Peter 1:2-4

Rejuvenation

Bless the Lord, O my soul, and all that is within me, bless His holy name.

Bless the Lord, O my soul, and forget not all His benefits;

Who forgives all your (my) iniquities,

Who heals all your (my) diseases;

Who redeems your (my) life from destruction,

Who crowns you (me) with lovingkindness and tender mercies,

Who satisfies your (my) mouth with good things,

So that your (my) youth is renewed like the eagle.

—Psalm 103:1-5

In Jesus' name I decree that my youth is renewed like the eagle as I am renewed in the spirit of my mind. I watch over my heart with all diligence because from it flows the issues of life. What I allow in my mind and heart affects my body and the state of my life. Therefore my body is rejuvenating daily because I am focused on the truth, goodness, and great benefits of the Lord.

I do not allow sin to enter my life, and therefore the consequence of sin (which is the spirit of death that oppresses the body and mind) has no hold on me. If I do sin, I repent and am forgiven and cleansed from all unrighteousness, guilt, condemnation, and shame because of Christ's great mercy. My body is completely free from the destructive power of sin. The law of the spirit of life in Christ Jesus has set me free from the law of sin and death. I do not allow unforgiveness, bitterness, or offense to have place in my life. Therefore, my life and body are free from these destructive contaminants.

Jesus is Life and Light. The words He speaks are spirit and life. Therefore I am filled afresh with His ageless, eternal Life and Light when I focus on Him and drink of His promises, declaring their power into my body, soul, and spirit.

In Jesus' name I call forth His Spirit, Life, and Light to fill every cell, organ, and fiber of my being. I meditate on His Spirit, Life and Light filling my mind, emotions, organs in the head, neck, chest, abdomen, back, legs, arms, feet, and hands. Come Spirit, Life and Light of Christ. Fill me. Renew me. I speak renewal through the power of Jesus into every organ of my body.

I speak to my skin (the largest organ of my body), and command rejuvenation and elasticity to be restored to every cell of it. "Skin, receive the glory of God in Jesus' name." I call forth the glory of God to arise, shine, and appear on me as Isaiah prophesied and as was seen on both Jesus and Moses.

I speak to my sight and hearing in the name of Jesus and call forth excellence and precision into these organs of my body. I command health and strength to all my bones, muscles, tendons, and joints. I decree that my heart and circulatory system are strong and healthy. My lungs and respiratory system are vibrant in Christ, functioning at optimum levels of performance. In Christ's name, I speak health and rejuvenation to all the digestive, endocrine, hormonal, immune, reproductive, nerve, electrical, and elimination organs of my body.

I care for my mind and emotions and, as a result, I think only on those things that are true, honorable, right, pure, good, lovely and all that is of good report. I am anxious for nothing because I submit to the Lord all that concerns me. I reject negative thoughts and emotions and cast all my cares upon Him because He cares for me. As a result, my body, mind, and emotions have no stress – only peace. I am kept in perfect peace because I set my mind and heart on Him. I have the mind of Christ, and my thinking processes are sharp. My youth is renewed daily in Christ. I abide in Him and His Life flows in and through me.

When I am weary, God increases strength in me. When I lack might, He increases power. I run and do not get weary. I walk and do not faint, for the Lord renews my strength when I wait on Him. I mount up with wings like the eagle.

I always yield fruit and will be full of fresh vision all the days of my life. Like Caleb, I will still be pursuing the fulfillment of God-given destiny after 85 years of age, being full of life, energy and ability.

I soak in His presence and glory. I receive refreshment and impartation into every part of my being. Blessed be the name of the Lord who renews and rejuvenates my body, soul, and spirit daily! As my days are, so shall my strength be. I am fully satisfied in Christ all the days of my life.

Scripture References:
Exodus 34:30; Joshua 14:11; Psalm 92:14; 103:1-5; Proverbs 4:23; Isaiah 1:1-2; 26:3; 40:29-31; Matthew 17:2; John 1:9; 6:63; 7:37; 8:12; 9:5; 14:6; Romans 6:23; 8:2; 1 Corinthians 2:16; Ephesians 4:23; Philippians 4:6-8; 1 Peter 5:7

I Am Supernatural in Christ

*I*n Jesus, I am a new creation. Through the Holy Spirit I am able to do all the works that Jesus did, and even greater works. I am a supernatural being because of my new birth in Christ. In my spirit man, I am fully righteous and made in the image and likeness of Christ. His nature and character have been given to me. His power and glory have been given to me. By Christ's amazing promises and grace, I am filled with all that He is and all that He has.

Miracles, signs and wonders follow me when I preach the good news of the Kingdom, for the Lord Himself confirms the Word I proclaim. In the glorious name of Jesus, I create light in the darkness and order in chaos by calling those things that are not as though they are. In Christ, I have power over all the works of the enemy and nothing harms me. The strongholds of sickness, disease, oppression, possession, and demonic attack are under my feet when I take dominion in Christ. I go forth in the mighty name of Jesus that is more powerful and carries more authority than any other name.

The invisible realm of the Kingdom of God has been granted to me through the eternal, unbreakable covenant that Christ made on my behalf. My heavenly Father has chosen gladly to give me the Kingdom. I have access to the throne room and the heavenly realms by faith through the blood of Christ. I enter with boldness and confidence before the throne of grace and obtain grace and mercy to help in time of need.

The eyes of my heart and understanding are opened by the Spirit of God, so that I will know the hope of my calling in Christ. The God of my Lord Jesus Christ, the Father of glory, gives me the spirit of wisdom and of revelation in the knowledge of the Godhead and opens my understanding to know the surpassing greatness of Christ's power toward me and to all who believe. These are in accordance with the working of the strength of His might. I am seated with Christ at the right hand of the Father in heavenly places, far above all rule and authority and power and dominion, and every name that is named not only in this age but also in the one to come.

Through Christ, I have come to the city of the living God, the heavenly Jerusalem, and to myriads of angels, to the general assembly and church of the firstborn who are enrolled in heaven, and to God, the Judge of all, and to the spirits of the righteous made perfect, and to Jesus, the mediator of a new covenant, and to the sprinkled blood, which speaks better than the blood of Abel.

I have received a kingdom that cannot be shaken and therefore I show gratitude by which I may offer to God an acceptable service with reverence and awe. My God is a consuming fire.

I am an eternal being, and Eternal Life dwells within me. Therefore, I am not limited to the restraints of time and distance. As the Spirit leads, I can perform supernatural acts like Jesus did, such as walking on water, walking through walls, feeding multitudes with miraculous provision, changing substance like water to wine, altering weather patterns, being lifted up off the earth, raising the dead, and working extraordinary miracles.

Angels are dispatched into divine assignments when I declare the Word of God, for they obey the voice of the Lord's Word that I speak! The words of Jesus are spirit and life. Angels ascend and descend upon me because Christ dwells in me. They are ministering spirits sent by God to help me in my mission on the earth. Even when I do not sense them or see them, they are with me to protect me and minister to me.

As a supernatural being, my senses are exercised to discern good and evil – and I choose good. I am able to see, hear, and feel the invisible Kingdom realm around me.

I am the temple of the Holy Spirit. My being is filled with glory when I remember and proclaim the goodness of God. The Lord is good and His mercy endures forever. Because Christ dwells in me, I live under the open heaven, and blessings come upon me and overtake me. I am blessed with every spiritual blessing in the heavenly places in Christ.

I am a supernatural being encountering Christ and His Kingdom. I bring glory to God through my obedience to Him and by the word of my testimony.

Scripture References:
Genesis 1:1-3; Deuteronomy 28:1-2; 2 Kings 6:15-17; 2 Chronicles 5:13-14; Psalm 91:11-13; 103:20; Matthew 8:23-27; 10:7-8; 14:22-29; Mark 6:33-44; 16:20; Luke 10:19; 12:32; John 1:51; 2:1-10; 3:16; 6:63; 10:27; 14:12; 17:22; 20:19; Acts 1:9; 19:11; Romans 4:17; 8:14; 1 Corinthians 3:16; 2 Corinthians 5:17,21; Ephesians 1:3; 1:17-20, 2:6; Philippians 2:9-10; Hebrews 1:14; 5:14; 4:16; 10:19-22; 12:22-24, 28-29; 2 Peter 1:3-4; Revelation 12:11

12 Decrees for
Your Nation

*I*n Jesus' name, I decree that my nation is turning to God and is embracing the truth of His Word.

In Jesus' name, I decree that the active, holy, and powerful conviction of the Holy Spirit is visiting every individual in my nation, drawing souls into true encounter with Christ.

In Jesus' name, I decree that all who serve the nation in government positions are visited by the righteousness, truth, and justice of God, and that they live in the fullness of Christ's wisdom in all they do. I decree that any corruption in government will be exposed and dealt with in wisdom and righteousness in order for the nation to be cleansed.

In Jesus' name, I decree that the education leaders, systems, and institutions in my nation are being filled with Kingdom values, wisdom, conviction, and truth.

In Jesus' name, I decree that the body of Christ in my nation is actively walking with and serving the Lord with fullness of focus, sincerity of faith and in the demonstration of the power of the Spirit.

In Jesus' name, I decree that those who live in my nation are kept in good health and are offered excellent health services and care. I decree that all will live in the health and strength of the Lord.

In Jesus' name, I decree that the media in my nation communicates godly morals and values, and that the gospel is favored in media.

In Jesus' name, I decree that every godly business and enterprise flourishes in my nation and every corrupt business and enterprise is exposed and falls. I decree prosperity and fruitfulness in my nation as a result of godliness, in order for every individual to have all they need.

In Jesus' name, I decree that the marriages and families in my nation are blessed with love, joy, and peace and that every home is filled with the goodness of God.

In Jesus' name, I decree that the body of Christ is mobilized into the harvest fields of my nation to bring forth much fruit.

In Jesus' name, I decree that righteousness thrives in my nation in every realm of life and that lawlessness and corruption have no place.

JESUS IS LORD OVER MY NATION!

Power of Prayer

*M*y prayers are powerful. Every prayer I pray that is according to the will of God is granted to me. When I pray, I believe that I have received and I have the request that I asked of Him.

My heavenly Father answers every prayer I pray in the Name of Jesus so that my joy will be full. When I ask of my Heavenly Father, I ask in faith, with no doubting, for all things are possible to those who believe.

Scriptural References:
Mark 9:23; 11:24 ; John 15:16; 16:24; James 1:5-6;
1 John 5:14-15

My Prayer List

Date of Prayer	Request	Scripture Promise	Date Answered

Notes:

_____

_____

_____

_____

_____

_____

My Prayer List

Date of Prayer	Request	Scripture Promise	Date Answered

Notes:

_____

_____

_____

_____

_____

My Prayer List

Date of Prayer	Request	Scripture Promise	Date Answered

Notes:

My Prayer List

Date of Prayer	Request	Scripture Promise	Date Answered

Notes:

_____

_____

_____

_____

_____

_____

Personal Decrees

Personal Decrees

Personal Decrees

Personal Decrees

Personal Decrees

Personal Decrees

Personal Decrees

About Patricia King

Patricia King is a respected apostolic minister of the gospel and has been a pioneering voice in ministry, serving for over 30 years as a Christian minister in conference speaking, prophetic service, church leadership, and television and radio appearances. She is the founder of Patricia King Ministries, Women in Ministry Network and Patricia King Institute, the co-founder of XPmedia.com, and director of Women on the Frontlines. She has written many books, produced numerous CDs and DVDs, and hosts her TV program, *Patricia King – Everlasting Love TV*. She is also a successful business owner and an inventive entrepreneur. Patricia's reputation in the Christian community is world-renowned.

To Connect:

Patricia King website: PatriciaKing.com

Facebook: Facebook.com/PatriciaKingPage

Patricia King Institute: PatriciaKingInstitute.com

Women on the Frontlines and Women in Ministry Network: Woflglobal.com

Patricia King – Everlasting Love TV show and many other video teachings by Patricia: XPmedia.com

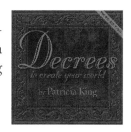

DON'T STOP BEFORE YOU ARE FINISHED

God's plan is for you to prosper and be in health, even as your soul prospers (3 John 2 KJV). He wants you to be fruitful and to increase and multiply in every good thing. This brings glory to Him.

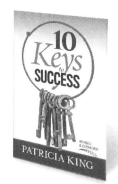

10 Keys to Success offers you valuable insights taken from the lives of two of the most successful persons in the Bible. Then discover 10 effective and proven principles found in Scripture keys that open doors to the success God wants you to have.

STEP INTO THE BLESSING ZONE

You were created to be blessed, to know the very best that God has to offer all the days of your life. If you have been living in a place of lack, hardship, or frustration, it is time to shift into the blessing zone and know the goodness of God in every area of your life!

Patricia shares divine secrets of how you can step out of simply living day-to-day and live *In the Zone!*

CREATED TO KNOW ABUNDANCE

You were not created for poverty or financial devastation. You were created to know abundance and blessing. Patricia shares insights from Scripture, testimonies, revelation, and biblical principles that outline how you can cooperate with God's promise for abundance and blessing. Step out of financial struggle and enter into miraculous provision and supernatural supply!

YOU HAVE SUPERNATURAL SENSES

Just as He gave us five natural senses, God also created us with five spiritual senses. Cultivate your spiritual senses and learn how to see, hear, feel, taste and smell more of the supernatural realm that is all around you.

This book is is a doorway to encounters that will answer the cry of your heart to know Him and His Kingdom more fully and intimately.

YOU'VE BEEN GIVEN EARS THAT HEAR

Do you desire to hear what God is saying in this hour? Are you crying out for the Lord to speak to you about the deep mysteries of His kingdom? Do you wonder what His plans are for your life? Then you need ears that hear!

In *Ears that Hear,* you will come to know that you too, can hear God's voice. You will learn simple and practical ways to step into the prophetic and to begin listening to what the Lord is saying.

YOU'VE BEEN GIVEN EYES THAT SEE

Do you desire to see into the unseen realm? Are you longing to gaze upon Jesus and His Kingdom? Then you need eyes that see!

Eyes that See will help you lay hold of the spiritual sight that you have been given in Christ. You will see in Scripture that the Lord has opened your eyes, and you will learn simple and practical ways to begin to practice seeing in the Spirit.

RECEIVE A GLORIOUS REVELATION

Discover a path of miracle replenishment and increase in everything that pertains to you – your physical strength, your love, your time, your provision, your gifts, your anointing, and anything else that flows from you to God and others.

Receive this God-given revelation through biblical examples, insights and keys, along with practical applications, personal testimonies, and decrees for activation.

EXPERIENCE FINANCIAL BREAKTHROUGH

You were created to know abundance and blessing. Not only is God well able to prosper His people, but He has given us the tools to lay hold of abundance right now. Patricia opens your eyes to God's prosperity plan for you and gives you powerful Scripture-based decrees to open heaven's windows of blessing over your life.

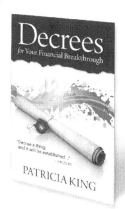

The Word of God never returns void; it always produces fruit. Grab hold of these decrees and get your financial breakthrough!

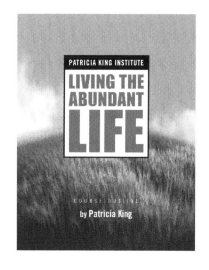

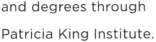

Additional copies of this book and other
book titles from Patricia King are available at:

Amazon.com
PatriciaKing.com

Bulk/wholesale prices for stores and ministries:

Please contact: resource@patriciaking.com

Patricia King Enterprises

Manufactured by Amazon.ca
Bolton, ON